THE HISTORY OF PHYSICAL CULTURE

THE HISTORY OF PHYSICAL CULTURE

CONOR HEFFERNAN

First published in 2022
as part of the *Sport and Society* Book Imprint
doi: 10.18848/978-1-957792-23-1/CGP (Full Book)

Common Ground Research Networks
University of Illinois Research Park
2001 South First St, Suite 201 L
Champaign, IL 61820

Copyright © [Conor Heffernan] 2022

All rights reserved. Apart from fair dealing for the purposes of study, research, criticism or review as permitted under the applicable copyright legislation, no part of this book may be reproduced by any process without written permission from the publisher.

Library of Congress Cataloging-in-Publication Data

Names: Heffernan, Conor, author.
Title: The history of physical culture / Conor Heffernan.
Description: Champaign, Illinois : Common Ground Research Networks, 2022. |
  Series: Sport & Society Teaching Pocketbook Series ; vol. 2 | Includes
  bibliographical references. | Summary: "This book provides an engaged
  and accessible historical overview of physical culture from the Ancient
  World to the Modern Day. In it, readers are introduced to the training
  practices of Ancient Greece, India, and China among other areas. From
  there, the book explores the evolution of exercise systems and messages
  in the Western World with reference to three distinct epochs: the
  Middles Ages and Renaissance, the Enlightenment, and its aftermath and
  the nineteenth to the present day. Throughout the book, attention is
  drawn not only to how societies exercised, but why they did so. The
  purpose of this book is to provide those new to the field of physical
  culture an historical overview of some of the major trends and
  developments in exercise practices. Here both the exercise systems, and
  their meanings are studied"-- Provided by publisher.
Identifiers: LCCN 2022041816 (print) | LCCN 2022041817 (ebook) | ISBN
  9781957792224 (paperback) | ISBN 9781957792231 (pdf)
Subjects: LCSH: Physical education and training--History. |
  Exercise--History.
Classification: LCC GV211 .H44 2022 (print) | LCC GV211 (ebook) | DDC
  796.071--dc23/eng/20221006
LC record available at https://lccn.loc.gov/2022041816
LC ebook record available at https://lccn.loc.gov/2022041817

SPORT & SOCIETY POCKETBOOK TEACHING SERIES

The **Sport and Society Pocketbook Teaching Series** aims to introduce students and a general readership to relevant topics, theories, and concepts within sport history and sport sociology. The topics will vary but are united in their purpose to serve as an accessible alternative to generic textbook offerings or academic research monographs. We hope that the shorter and more accessible pocketbook format of the series will mean that each book can be read in an hour or two on a quiet evening or while commuting on a bus or train. This aligns with our ethos of accessibility in scholarly communication.

Books in the series can be accessed in print and electronic formats. In addition, and in parallel to both editions, each title will be accompanied by an online repository where additional learning and teaching resources are provided. The electronic platform for the series will include links to recent and significant research articles, visual materials, podcasts, lectures, and more, thus securing ongoing relevance by providing new and engaging resources and perspectives aligned with the topic of each book.

This series is for teachers, learners, and individuals with an interest in sports alike.

Dr. Jörg Krieger (Aarhus University, Denmark)
Dr. April Henning (University of Stirling, United Kingdom)
Dr. Lindsay Parks Pieper (University of Lynchburg, United States)
Dr. Jesper Andreasson (Linnaeus University, Sweden)

A link to access additional online resources is provided at:
https://doi.org/10.18848/978-1-957792-23-1/CGP

TABLE OF CONTENTS

Introduction	*1*
Ancient Physical Culture(s)	9
Disappearance and Re-Emergence	29
The Birth of Physical Culture	51
The Age of Fitness	77
Conclusion	101
Notes	*109*

ACKNOWLEDGEMENT

My thanks first to the series editors for providing me with such a wonderful opportunity. I never had any intention of creating a book of this kind given the enormity of the task. Their confidence and support was truly valued. Professor Jan Todd, implicitly and explicitly, shaped this work. As always I owe a debt to Jan as both a friend and a mentor. Finally my love and appreciate to my parents, Susan and, the latest addition to our family, Cuán. Sorry for boring you all during his first few months on Earth.

INTRODUCTION

Why do people exercise? Where and how do they do it? More importantly why do *you* exercise? Have you ever considered the social, economic, and political reasons which support your ability to workout, get stronger and change your body?

Strange as these questions may seem, a great deal of thought has gone into answering them. Historians, sociologists, anthropologists, and any other number of experts have attempted to trace the human interest in lifting weights, stretching, training their bodies, dieting, and building their muscles. What they have learned is that, alongside sport, exercising one's body has a long and varied history. At one point in time, exercisers were predominately soldiers, athletes, patients recovering from illness and, occasionally, political leaders. Who exercised, and why, has undergone constant changes.

Beginning in the nineteenth century, the practice of going the gym, lifting weights, undertaking aerobic exercises or group exercise classes has become a popular activity for the public. Arguably it was only in the second half of the twentieth century that the public began to truly carve out time for exercise in a major way. We can learn a lot about different societies, and eras, by examining why people trained their bodies and for what reasons. A Spartan soldier in Ancient Greece may have used exercises similar to those found in a modern health club but the motivations differed greatly. One was done for warfare, the other for health.

How people exercise has changed dramatically in the last hundred years and although exercise is found at multiple points in human history, there is no denying that the modern age is defined by health cultures. You likely have access to a gym on your college campus or high school, in a nearby sports center, at a commercial gym or studio, in a hotel or even, for some lucky travelers, in an airport.

Modern exercisers often take for granted how accessible training has become. They also take for granted the reasons behind how and why we exercise. This small introduction to physical culture is driven by the belief that exercise, and the study of exercise, can tell us a great deal about human societies. Notice that I've written exercise, rather than sport. Although the two are closely related, sport exists in a different world to the kind of exercise discussed in this book.

What defines a sport? Speaking broadly, we could say competition, defined rules, score keeping, officiating, points, medals, etc. Exercise, or the kind of exercise one does in a gym, studio or at home, is often defined by strengthening the body, building muscle, losing weight, building cardiovascular health, rehabilitating muscle and yes, looking better aesthetically. Exercise is, however, a very vague term.

When people exercise, they may call themselves bodybuilders, powerlifters, weightlifters, Crossfitters, joggers, yogis and any manner of wonderful names. We may also use terms like 'keep fit,' 'toning,' 'shaping,' 'sculpting,' and, in the case of some enthusiastic bodybuilders, 'blasting.' Fun as these words are, they are rather imprecise. What makes things more confusing is how many words people have used to describe this kind of exercise in other parts of human history. What is now considered weightlifting was once called gymnastics or calisthenics. Likewise, bodybuilding was labelled physical culture for many decades.

Defining Physical Culture

The point of all this word play is to highlight the fact that it can often be difficult to accurately describe a society's, or a person's, interest in exercise. One of the most common terms used by academics, and the term that this handbook will be using, is *physical culture*. As per the H.J. Lutcher Stark Center of Physical Culture and Sports, physical culture will be understood here as 'the various activities people have employed over the centuries to strengthen their bodies, enhance their physiques, increase their endurance, enhance their health, fight against aging, and become better athletes.'[1] It is useful to think of sport and exercise as two similar activities (both train the body) but ones which exist in different worlds.

Professor Jan Todd previously used the term purposive exercise to describe the process whereby individuals apply structured methods to achieve 'specific physiological and philosophical goals.'[2] *Purposive exercise* underpins the practice of physical culture. Put another way physical culture means the changing of the body (making it stronger, leaner, faster, etc.) through some form of dedicated health program (i.e. exercising, stretching, dieting, etc.).

Why scholars have settled on the term physical culture is a topic for a different book, but it is important to note that the term physical culture was once the most popular way of describing one's health activities. Indeed, before competitive sport became an acceptable form of physical education, gymnastic drills and other forms of physical culture were regarded as physical education in most universities and schools.

Beginning in the mid nineteenth-century and continuing to the mid-twentieth-century, exercisers, physicians, physical educators, and politicians continually used the term physical culture when describing their health practices.[3] Saying 'I am a physical culturist' was the equivalent of now saying 'I am a bodybuilder' or 'I am a weightlifter.'

> ### Are You a Physical Culturist?
>
> Beginning in the mid 1800s exercisers referred to themselves as physical culturists when they engaged in some of the following activities: weightlifting, calisthenics, yoga, exercise classes, or walking. Would you be a physical culturist?
>
> How do we describe our behaviors today? Do you describe yourself as an exerciser or are you more specific i.e., I jog, I do Zumba classes, I go to the gym, etc.

Physical culture was replaced as a label in the 1920s and 1930s when exercisers began to use much more specific words to describe their interests. Nevertheless, it is still used by academics because it provides a useful way of

- Describing a society's interest in *purposive exercise*
- Comparing different societies
- Avoiding confusion with modern terms like weightlifting, yoga, Zumba, etc.

We will be using the term physical culture in this handbook precisely because it is so malleable. Covering over two thousand years of human history, we will need to be flexible in our thinking. Physical culture will be used to understand the various ways a society exercises and the reasons why they do so. As a working definition we will take physical culture to mean the ways people physically developed the body.

At this point, I want you to reflect on why people (or even why you) train their bodies. Over the past two thousand years, people have exercised to:

- Become better soldiers
- Move closer to God/Increase their spirituality
- Improve their health
- Overcome an illness
- Improve their appearance
- Lose weight
- Rehabilitate from an injury
- Become better parents
- Birth healthier children
- Prove their right to govern
- Become better students
- Keep their jobs
- Get stronger
- Improve sporting performance
- Unwind from too much stress
- Reverse/Slow old age
- To feel socially accepted by peers

These are just some of the reasons why people have exercised across history. How many of them underpin your own, or a friend's, interest in exercise? Also reflect on how people's motivations may change over time. Jack Lalanne, an American fitness expert and celebrity from the mid-twentieth-century exhibits this nicely.

Born in 1914, Lalanne began lifting weights as a teenager to improve his health and overcome his many illnesses. As he became stronger, Lalanne's motivations switched from health to bodybuilding. He opened his first gym in 1936 and worked through the 1940s coaching individuals. He even directed physical training for the US Navy during the Second World War. Lalanne was offered the opportunity to host a television fitness show in 1953 which ran for 34 years. Exercising thus became a means of keeping his job. Finally, Lalanne became a figurehead for those seeking to use exercise to slow down the aging process. His final books focused on living a long life, eating nutritious food and the role of exercise in preventing disease.[4] As Lalanne got older, and his opportunities expanded, his motivations changed.

You do not have to be Jack Lalanne to realize that the motivations for exercise are many, and often change. In your own life think about why people exercise and how this may have changed for you.

Structure

Now with this in mind, let's talk about this book. This book has two simple goals. The first is to discuss the history of physical culture and the second is to highlight the many meanings of exercise in human society. The second goal will be realized as you progress through this book. How this book is structured will help to achieve the first goal. Time, then, to discuss the roadmap or the structure for this book.

Chapter One examines the variety of physical cultures that existed in the Ancient World. Here we will be introduced to the exercise practices of societies in India, Egypt, Greece, and China among other regions. Attention will be drawn to the exercises done in these societies and the reasons why they were done. This Chapter will look at the ancient gymnasium, the role of exercise in military cultures and the tentative origins of fitness as we understand the term.

Chapter Two discusses the 'disappearance' of physical culture in Europe during the Middle Ages (fifth to thirteenth century) and its re-emergence during the Renaissance (fourteenth to sixteenth century) and Enlightenment (seventeenth and eighteenth century) period. After the fall of the Roman Empire in fifth century, many of the gymnasium cultures of the Ancient World were no longer popular in the Western world. They were eventually 'rediscovered' in later centuries as people began to take an interest once more in training the body. How and why, this occurred, and the importance of this rediscovery, are explored here.

Having 'rediscovered' physical culture by the eighteenth-century, Chapter Three explores the intensification in interest in physical culture in Europe, America, and the colonial world. This period marked the effective beginning of the modern health and fitness industry (and was usefully described by contemporaries as the physical culture age). This Chapter opens with a discussion of nineteenth century physical culture and finishes just prior to the Second World War. Here we will look at the formalization of sports like bodybuilding and weightlifting while also discussing the emergence of the modern-day gym. Chapter Three ends just prior to the Second World War.

Chapter Four, covers 1945 to the present day. Although studying a shorter period than previous Chapters, this time nevertheless encapsulates several new and emerging trends within the field of physical culture. Here, we will cover the general acceptance of fitness in the modern age, as well as the cultural impact of muscles in American and European media from the 1980s to the present day. Additionally, we will get the opportunity to discuss the democratization of fitness which occurred in the second half of the twentieth century wherein more trainees took to different forms of physical culture.

We will finish the handbook with a short conclusion reminding us of the key themes discussed in this book.

How to Read This Handbook

How to read a book is rarely discussed. After all, reading is a relatively straightforward process. Begin at page one and read until the end. My hope for this handbook is that it can be read and used in a variety of ways. For those seeking a broad overview of physical culture or the history of fitness, please do begin at the start and work your way through. For others seeking information about a specific period, or a specific individual, I am hopeful that the Chapters lend themselves to 'bite size' reading. Use the book as a reference guide, one which can help answer a nagging question, introduce you to a new history, or something that can inform an essay question. This book, like the exercises and practices it discusses, exists for many different purposes. Please use the one which suits your interests, and your needs, best.

CHAPTER 1

Ancient Physical Culture(s)

> *It is a disgrace to grow old through sheer carelessness before seeing what manner of man you may become by developing your bodily strength and beauty to their highest limit. But you cannot see that, if you are careless; for it will not come of its own accord.*
>
> Socrates, as quoted in Memorabilia.[1]

Written in roughly 371 BCE, the above quotation, attributed by Xenophon to the Greek philosopher Socrates, acts as a fantastic starting point on discussions of ancient physical cultures. On meeting his companion, Epigenes, who is in poor physical condition, Socrates lists the innumerable benefits of exercise. In the full dialogue, Socrates connected the strong and muscular body to the protection of one's home, the survival of one's city-state and heightened levels of thought. As Epigenes meekly protested that he could not exercise, Socrates intensified his argument. The meeting ended with a chastised Epigenes disappearing from the conversation.

Whether or not Socrates had this conversation with Epigenes is irrelevant, but, that it was written about Socrates rather than by Socrates is an important distinction. What is important about its subsequent record was the importance placed on abundant health. The modern interest in fitness has, as we will discuss in later Chapters, often been connected to the nineteenth century or indeed twentieth century. This does not mean, however, that those in the 'Ancient World' were not equally concerned with health, strength, and fitness.[2] Before we unpack this a little bit more, lets return to Socrates and his motivations for exercise.

In admonishing his friend, Socrates spoke about one's own health, city, and spirit. Physical culture in the Ancient World was done for many of the same reasons people exercise today. I have personally encountered Socrates' quote spray-painted on several walls in gyms around Europe and the United States. So, we may think that people have always exercised for the same reasons. We need to check these assumptions. Physical culture in the Ancient World was used in a variety of ways, and by a variety of groups.

To that end, this Chapter examines the history of physical culture in China, Egypt, India, Greece, and Rome. This is something of a 'whistle stop' tour of the Ancient World and is done to show both the breadth, and the variety, of exercise in ancient societies.

At this point it is worth acknowledging that a great deal of attention in later Chapters will be given exclusively to 'Western' physical cultures, by which I mean European or North American. This does not mean that rich practices and lineages did not exist in Africa, Asia, or South America but rather that physical culture scholars have tended to privilege Western histories. With that in mind, lets begin.

Ancient China

In a wonderfully engaging examination of Chinese physical cultures, Nigel B. Crowther found that weightlifting, archery, weight throwing, tug of war, boxing, and a host of other activities were practiced by Chinese men during the Han period (206 BCE–220 CE).[3] This is perhaps unsurprising given the long history of Chinese martial arts like kung fu.

What is less well known is the kinds of strength exercises and demonstrations done separately or in conjunction with military practices. Examining the period 6000 BCE to 1500 CE in China, Crowther cited religion, warfare, personal health, and social customs as the primary motivations for these men, and it was primarily men, to lift weights.

While Crowther focused predominately on male physical cultures there is some evidence of women engaging in forms of physical activity as a form of sport but also as physical training.[4] A common theme throughout this book will be the fact that female physical culture has always existed but has not always been well documented. When we move to Ancient Athens or Sparta, we will see a lot more information on women's physical culture.

Returning to Ancient China, we know that a great deal of time was dedicated by men to improving their strength and physical health. We also know that the two groups most likely to engage in these kinds of activities were soldiers and athletes. When it came to lifting weights, Chinese athletes did not disappoint. To display their strength, regional strongmen lifted rocks and metal objects, like heavy tripods and massive swords swung overhead or with one hand.[5]

As we will see, stone lifting was a common activity across the Ancient World and, due largely to its simplicity, is still practiced today. One's ability to lift such objects was often linked to their fighting prowess, virility and as an indication of their family's strength. Strength was not merely an object of vanity but instead something of considerable societal importance.

> ### What Does Strength Mean?
>
> In Ancient China, and in other parts of the Ancient World, strength displays were often linked to political celebrations, to religious devotion and even to funeral rites. For some cultures, the ability to lift a heavy object (most commonly a large stone) was done to prove one's manliness.
>
> What does strength mean in the modern era? Can you think of any religious, political, or gendered displays of strength?

Stone lifting was the primary way in which men competed in strength competitions with one another, but it was not the only avenue open to those seeking to build their vitality. During China's Warring States period (475–221 BCE), martial artists took part in a single or two man lift of a large three-legged cauldron called a *ding*. Significantly *dings* could weigh upwards of several hundred pounds and their irregular shape made lifting them more difficult.[6] Traditionally, and since the second millennium BCE, such cauldrons were used during ancestral worship rituals, which suggests that the ability to lift these cauldrons was symbolically important.

The lifting of stone objects, and symbolically important objects, continued well past the ancient period. Sport historian Zhi Dao's work on the history of sport in China found that rural strongmen during the Tang Dynasty (618 to 907 CE), lifted stone lions supposedly weighing close to 1,000 kilograms.[7] More realistically, we also have stories of performers completing back lifts with a dozen people on their back during this time. Lim SK has also cited the use of the *guandao* (a long pole with a 'moon blade' attached to one end) as a weightlifting practice from this period.[8]

The *guandao* was swung around the body in many Chinese martial arts. According to Lim, soldiers and strongmen in the Tang Dynasty swung heavy guandao around their bodies to build strength and muscle.[9] It was also done to show one's physical prowess. Remarkably, this practice, along with stone and *ding* lifting, still exists today. As a fun aside, when the World Strongest Man competition was held in Chengdu, China in 2005, contestants were forced to carry a *ding* for distance. The event reminded viewers of physical culture's long and varied history in the country.

Ancient Egypt

In ancient Egypt, weightlifting was an equally popular practice. Obviously, problems exist when discussing Ancient Egypt, namely that this label could be applied to a period covering thirty centuries! A rough timeline for Ancient Egypt is 3000 BCE to 300 CE. In 332 BC, Alexander the Great conquered Egypt and brought it under Greco-Roman rule. This is an important consideration as later Egyptian physical culture was greatly influenced by the gymnasium cultures of Greece and Roman discussed in later sections.[10]

In this section we are going to focus on distinctly Egyptian physical cultures from c. 1200 BCE, while acknowledging that gymnasiums inspired by Greco-Roman culture did come to Egypt in a very real way post-300 CE.[11] When studying physical culture from the nineteenth or twentieth century we can often rely on training manuals, newspapers, or memoirs for information. Such luxuries rarely exist from the Ancient World. Scholars studying sport and physical culture from this time have thus relied on things like paintings, poetry, murals, physical objects, and medical texts.

One of the primary ways scholars access Egyptian physical cultures are from murals found in tombs. The best-known example are the tombs at Beni Hasan, dating to the eleventh and twelfth century BCE. In these tombs, we have evidence of men, and at times women, exercising with weights, or though gymnastics, in the form of paintings.

The tomb of Khety, at Beni Hasan, depicted Egyptian men exercising with weights or strengthening their bodies through gymnastics and wrestling.[12] Such murals hint at both a recognition that strength training held value and that it was popular. That these activities were deemed worthy of painting indicates some level of societal respect for them.

Weightlifting appears to have been one of many sports engaged in by local soldiers, athletes, and men to improve their health in Egypt. If you go online, you'll even find some enthusiastic Egyptian nationalists claim that weightlifting was so popular and strong in Ancient Egypt that it spread from Egypt to far flung places like Rome, Greece, Cartage and Phoenicia.[13] Whether or not this is the case is debatable but various forms of physical culture existed. Wolfgang Decker, one of the leading sport historians of the ancient world, has even claimed that Ancient Egypt was the first documented athletic civilization![14]

Returning to physical culture, one of the most popular weightlifting techniques in Egypt was sack swinging which could be compared with the modern day snatch Olympic lift done with one hand. To build their bodies, and as a form of competition, individuals lifted a sack of sand with one hand and brought it overhead.

Images of sack swinging can be found in the Beni Hasan tomb.[15] Alongside weight training, we know that gymnastics was a hugely popular form of training for soldiers and citizens alike. Using a series of bodyweight or calisthenics exercise, men, and at times women, would strengthen their muscles, improve their agility, and engage in friendly (or competitive) games with one another.

In Ancient Egypt, there also existed the *Heb-Sed* festival. Created to celebrate the ruling King *(Pharaoh),* the *Heb-Sed* festival included an athletic component for the *Pharaoh.* Done to prove one's fitness to rule, Heb-Sed tests were typified by the ability to run through a special course. They were held after thirty years under the same political leader and then every three to four years. In essence *Pharaohs* were required to literally prove their fitness to rule.[16] The need to prove one's 'fitness to rule' dated to at least 3000 BCE and lasted for thousands of years. Here one gets a glimpse of the practical and symbolic importance of health in Ancient Egypt.

Ancient India

Some regions in Ancient India also boasted a fascinating strength culture which encompassed both athletic and military training for wrestlers and soldiers. Like Ancient Egypt, where heavy sacks were swung the most common form of training in Ancient India came in the form of heavy club swinging. India was not entirely unique in this regard, as Persia also boasted a rich history of heavy club *(meel)* swinging, but the popularity of the practice in India marks it out as unique.[17]

'Indian clubs,' as they're now known in Europe and North America, have made a resurgence in recent years as part of the functional training trend which has swept across gyms.[18] It is often common for Indian clubs to be called steel clubs in modern gyms. Unsurprisingly given what we now know about other cultures, training in Ancient India was similarly linked to warfare and religion.

While Indian clubs (or *joris* as they are commonly referred to) appeared in early Buddhist and Jain writings, their ancient past is best understood through Hindu texts like the *Mahabharata*, written between 400 BCE and 400 CE.[19] In the text, *gadas,* the heavy club precursors to Indian clubs, were mentioned at several points by the text's heroes and demons. Included among the *gada* users was Vishnu, one of the most revered Hindu deities.[20] In fact, it is said by some that Vishnu was responsible for forging the original *gada.* Vishnu's association with the *gada* meant that symbolically, it came to be linked with power, destruction, and a certain amount of reverence. Those who swung the *gada* or the Indian clubs, took the matter seriously.

Also relevant was Hanuman, an ape-like God, revered for his strength. A demigod praised for his devotion to Lord Rama, Hanuman is intensely related to Indian clubs in Hindu texts and iconography. As the Hindu God of wrestling, Hanuman explicitly linked Indian clubs with athleticism. This connection was reiterated daily for Indian exercisers, who for centuries, prayed to Hanuman before training in the gymnasium.[21] In Ancient Greece, Hercules was often the god found within the gymnasium. In India, it was Hanuman.

Reverence for Indian clubs stemmed from their military usefulness, and it is interesting to note that the *Mahabharata* was written soon after the Indian Vedic Age (1500–500 BCE) during which heavy clubs were often used in battle. Exercising with the

Indian club was both a form of physical culture and a means of training for battle.

The emergence of other weapons in the following centuries did little to displace the clubs' battlefield application, although such weapons did signal a change in the clubs' use. While still used in battle, Indian clubs became a training tool during the fifth century for wrestlers who combined club swinging with stone lifting and calisthenics to build their bodies.[22] Also stemming from this period were two Indian wrestling exercises still practiced by countless athletes today: *bethaks* (or the Hindu squat) and the *dand* (or the Hindu push up).

Other forms of equipment used were *nals* and *gar nals. Nals*, according to the anthropologist Joseph Alter, are the equivalent to the modern free weights found in gyms today.[23] Made of stone, these small implements were, and continue to be, used to develop the muscles of the shoulders and arms.

They are best imagined as stone dumbbells. *Gar nals*, on the other hand, resemble stone donuts that the exerciser places around their shoulders to train their legs. By placing their head through the 'hole' of the 'donut' the exerciser could engage in heavy squats to grow stronger.

In the Indian gymnasium or *akhara*, physical culture was a military practice, a form of religious devotion and a religious exercise. Just as the Ancient Greeks used gymnasiums, wrestlers used akharas, the term for their specified training spaces. Joseph Alter's work on contemporary wrestlers found that the exercises used trace back hundreds of years.[24]

Indeed, the club swinging exercises practiced by Indian wrestlers today are likely to have been very similar to their ancient counterparts. In swinging heavy *joris,* exercisers attempted to enter a meditative style trance wherein they could build their energy while simultaneously reviving their 'vital energies.' This was a holistic type of training which encompassed mind, body and spirit.

Another obvious physical culture in Ancient India was yoga. Although modern forms of yoga have their origins more so in nineteenth century exercise systems, but traditional yogic postures and exercises trace their origins to c. 500 BCE if not earlier.[25] We will return to forms of modern yoga in later Chapters, but it is important to stress here that traditional forms of yoga were far more rooted in religious practices than later iterations. The *Yogasutras of Patanjali* (c. 100 BCE) stated that *yogas chitta vritti nirodha* which can be roughly translated as yoga is the stilling of the fluctuations of the mind.[26] This is a very somewhat more meditative philosophy than is found is certain, modern, yoga studios which may focus more on physical health.

What is fascinating about Ancient Indian physical cultures, and this is also the case with Ancient Persian (modern day Iran), is that these exercises have persisted. In Ancient Persia, soldiers and athletes swung heavy clubs *(meels)* in the gym *(zurkhaneh)*. At the time of writing, it is still possible to train in a *zurkhaneh* where, nowadays, ancient methods are mixed with modern ones.[27] In India, Pakistan, and Bangladesh, *akharas* are still found and, in some areas, are thriving. It is worth noting this fact because, from here on, we will be devoting a great deal of attention to European and North American forms of physical culture.

This is not because European and North American physical culture is more interesting or more important than say, Chinese, Egyptian or Indian physical cultures but rather because European and North American physical culture became the preeminent systems used by exercisers from the eighteenth-century onwards. The reasons for this, which will be discussed in later Chapters, can be briefly attributed here to Western imperialism, colonization and, from the nineteenth century, globalization.

Ancient Greece

For exercisers in the West, the influence of Greco-Roman exercise over our own training systems is remarkably strong. How people trained in Ancient Greece helped inform exercisers in the 1800s, 1900s and now the 2000s. Part of the reason for this is simple, access to Greek materials was far more plentiful than other parts of the world, at least initially for Western eyes. Using a rough timeline, Ancient Greece will be used to define the period 1200 BCE to 323 CE.[28]

Like China, Egypt and India, regional and cultural differences existed in Ancient Greece. But Ancient Greece was not a 'real country.' Instead, it was a blanket term given to describe the landmass of Greece. What instead existed were hundreds of individual city-states, each with their own cultures and forms of government. Some, like Athens or Sparta, you likely know already. Because of these differences, we will content ourselves here with broad, but nevertheless true, generalizations.

In Ancient Greece, stone lifting, calisthenics, and rudimentary forms of dumbbell training were practiced by soldiers, athletes, patients, and a host of other groups to train their bodies.[29] We also have evidence of some limited female physical culture which we will soon discuss.

Exercise was of utmost value in Greek city-states, for numerous populations. Given that my initial, and many others' motivation for training, came from the movie *300* (released in 2006), it seems fitting to begin with military training. When talking about military training in Ancient Greece, the city-state of Sparta seems the most obvious choice. According to the classicist Humphrey Michell the Spartan training system was predicated on the need to, maintain an army of experts who were ready and able at any moment to suppress sedition within the state or repel invasion from without. The Spartan was a professional soldier and nothing else, and his education directed entirely to two ends - physical fitness and obedience to authority...[30]

Education was seen as a serious, disciplined undertaking. The mother instructed the young child, and the father supplemented this early teaching with moral training. At the age of 6 or 7, all male offspring in Sparta were required to continue their fitness programs. They were required to undergo roughly five years of gymnastics or calisthenics in conjunction with sport and military training. Recreational boxing, for example, was a common pastime where it was combined with sport and weightlifting to build the troops which defined Sparta's fierceness.

The historian Plutarch (c. 46–120 CE) claimed that Spartan children were given a hoplon, or military shields, weighing roughly 25 lbs., as part of their training. Before battles they were told they had two choices: return with the *hoplon* or return on the *hoplon*. This life and death attitude to fighting explains the strictness of their training regimens.[31]

Spartans, as is perhaps clear, took fitness seriously. For this reason they were known for their promotion of women's physical culture. In the seventh century BCE, King Lycurgus structured Spartan society along militaristic lines. Because of this both men and women were expected to be physically fit. According to the ancient historian Xenophon, Lycurgus 'decreed that the female sex ought to take bodily exercise no less than the male.'[32]

Lycurgus established running and strength competitions for women in the hope that physically fit women would produce healthy and strong children. Later accounts of Lycurgus' plans, as detailed by Jan Todd, noted his promotion of running, wrestling,

Ancient Physical Culture(s)

discus and javelin.[33] As Todd explained, many outside Sparta likely disapproved of their love of exercise. Others, however, viewed it as entirely appropriate. The Athenian philosopher Plato (c. 428 BCE-348 BCE), proposed that women should join men in the gymnasium.[34]

Sparta may have led the way in military training but when it came to athletic training, the Athenians were in a league of their own. Under the influence of Greek physicians, Athenian athletes undertook strict forms of physical training and dieting prior to contests like the Olympics or the Nemean Games. Athletes would spend roughly ten months preparing for the Olympic games, held every four years in Olympia.[35]

Clayton Miles Lehmann's work on Ancient Greek training found that training for the Olympic Games necessitated the need for specialized sport coaches, training camps and serious diets.[36] During the last month of training, athletes would begin using *halteres* or stone dumbbells to build their speed and strength. Amazingly long jumpers would also use *halteres* during their jumps to increase the length of their feats.

Returning to the Nigel Crowther – whose research on China we have already discussed – he found that *halteres* typically weighed anywhere from 5 to 12 pounds and were used to strengthen the shoulders and arms as well as the legs. They served athletes, soldiers and the general trainee.[37] As an aside the term *halteres* is still used in certain European countries to denote dumbbells or weightlifting. For many years the French Weightlifting Federation was the *Fédération Française de Poids et Haltères.* This name acts as a small breadcrumb, leading us from the twentieth century to the Ancient World.

The Olympics, held every four years, were part of the great panhellenic sporting cycle that featured four large spectacles – the Olympic games, the Pythian games, the Nemean games and the Isthmian games. Held in conjunction with the Olympic games were the Heraean games, a footrace for women.[38] According to Pausania (110 CE–180 CE), the 'games consist of footraces for maidens. These are not all the same age. The first to run are the youngest; after them come the next in age, and the last to run are the oldest of the maidens.'[39]

The Hearaean games were perhaps the most obvious example of women's exercise in Athens but evidence exists of similar races being held for the goddess Artemis. Studying the remains of pottery shards found at Brauron historian, Allen Guttman noted that at least one depiction of a female runner had 'the muscular physique and long stride of a modern athlete.'[40] The issue of surviving sources, and whose history is written, is a persistent issue in studies of female strength and sport. What remains is nevertheless illuminating as to both sexes exercising habits.

Where people train is almost as important as to how they train. It is somewhat trite to point out that sport cannot take place without playing fields or courts. Likewise, physical training is often difficult without a space to train. Like the Indian wrestlers, discussed above, who used *akharas* to train, Greek city states regularly included *gymnasiums* as spaces for athletes to train. The word gymnasium itself is derived from *gumnazo*, meaning exercise, and gumnos, meaning naked. Breaking down the name in this way gives you an idea of what people did – or did not – wear when exercising in the *gymnasium*.

Gymnasiums were the location where trainers were found, exercise equipment was held and recovery in the form of massages or baths was undertaken. *Gymnasiums* were public buildings, municipally owned and controlled. They played a prominent role in Greek city states. They were common buildings and were often attached to stadiums when possible.

Gymnasiums began as athletic spaces for athletes, young men and soldiers to change their bodies. This, incidentally, included stretching for health (which many may view as a modern phenomenon).[41] Over time, they evolved into educational spaces for teenage boys and men. In an article on the Greek gymnasium in 1945, classicist Clarence A. Forbes depicted the gymnasium as 'a headquarters of higher and adult education.'[42]

The rooted custom of daily exercise and a bath brought men to the *gymnasium*. Once there, and in the company of like-minded individuals, *gymnasiums* became a place for social, and, at times, sexual intercourse, small talk, relaxation, lounging, a place to disseminate news, and a place to learn. What began as an ancient sports center evolved into an educational academy and social hub.

The Sophists, a Greek philosophical school most prominent in the fifth and fourth centuries BCE, were the first group to begin using the *gymnasium* as a lecture hall on a regularly basis. Others soon began to emulate the Sophists including Socrates, who made the *gymnasium* his home base. Gymnasiums were the universities of their time.

It was for this reason that so many Athenian philosophers, from Plato to Aristotle, stressed the importance of an education spanning mental exertion and physical exercise ('healthy mind/ healthy body'). Greek education, as conducted from roughly the fourth century onward, spanned physical exercise and traditional learning. Physical and mental health worked in tandem in Ancient Greece.

Athenian appreciation of the developed body even extended to male beauty contests which have been likened, at times, to early bodybuilding shows. But what of Greek strongmen? Given the importance of Hercules in Greek mythology, it would be remiss not to mention Ancient Greek strongmen.

Milo of Kroton, the sixth-century BCE athlete, is often credited with inventing progressive strength training. As a young man,

Milo dreamed of Olympic glory. To that end, he reputedly carried a young bull on his shoulders every day for four years. As the bull grew older and larger, Milo's strength increased.[43] This is a fanciful tale, there is no evidence Milo did this, but the story is regularly told even today to discuss the logic of progressive weight training. Milo did, however, supposedly walk a distance at Olympia with a young bull across his shoulders.[44]

Away from Greek mythology and storytelling, surviving artifacts suggest that athletes exhibited tremendous forms of strength and muscularity. A black volcanic rock, found on the island of Thera, which measures between 2-18m (7.15 feet) and 1-90m (6.23 feet) in circumference and weighs 479 kg (1058 lbs.), bears the inscription that 'Eumastas, son of Critobulus, lifted me from the ground. Sandstone blocks from Olympia, weighing 315 lbs., were said to have been lifted by Bybon and thrown with one hand. In the fourth-century CE, Jerome described weightlifting with metal balls instead of boulders. Taken together, such stories and records indicate the value placed on the trained body, and lifting, in ancient Greece.[45]

Ancient Rome

In 146 BCE the Romans conquered the Greek peninsula. With that, the seat of social and political importance in Europe shifted towards Rome. Rome, much like Ancient Greece, displayed a huge interest in physical training and gymnastics cultures.

To answer what is no doubt a burning question. Yes, we will begin with gladiators but specifically with debunking gladiatorial myths. Gladiators were the athletic superstars of their time. They were often highly trained fighters who competed against one another, or against animals, in the amphitheater. The amphitheater readers are most likely aware of is the Colosseum in Rome (which was completed in 80 CE).

While it seems that Gladiators did initially fight to the death, they eventually evolved into athletes. There is some debate among ancient Roman historians as to the origins of gladiators. Nicolaus of Damascus (64 BCE–4 CE) traced their origins to the Etruscans (900 BC–27 BC), an ancient society which assimilated with the Romans in the fourth century BCE.[46] Livy (59 BCE–17 AD), on the other had argued that the first gladiatorial fights dated to 310 BCE.[47]

Regardless of their origins, it is generally accepted that the first gladiatorial games, in which gladiators fought to the death, originated in 264 BCE when Decimus Junius Brutus created the games to honor his dead father.[48] What originally began as a funeral rite, evolved into a religious festival to honor both the gods and the deceased. What slowly phased out, however, was the fight to the death.

Following the Spartacus slave revolt against Roman rule in 73 BCE, gladiatorial combat became slightly more sanitized. Combatants did still fight to the death, but a new trained class of gladiators emerged. Many were not prisoners of war, as the original gladiartors had been, but were, in fact, free men attracted to the spectacle of fighting.[49]

Gladiators trained in specific training camps where a mixture of calisthenics and weight training would prepare them for battle. This was combined with a largely vegetarian diet, and 'sport psychology' sessions to create the ultimate fighters.[50] These sessions, as Donald Kyle explained, were designed to train the gladiators to accept potential death in the amphitheater.

There is also, as Anna McCullough and others found, evidence of female gladiators competing in the amphitheater, although the remaining historical evidence is often patchy at best. Senate decrees from 11 and 19 CE note the appearance of female gladiators, as do later literary texts from Roman poets like Juvenal (1–2 CE).[51]

Juvenal was somewhat sardonic in his comments on female gladiators, writing, 'what modesty can you expect in a woman who wears a helmet, abjures her own sex, and delights in feats of strength?'[52] Archaeologists have also discovered remains of Roman women believed to be gladiators.[53]

But physical culture in Ancient Rome meant more than just gladiatorial bouts. There was also a continuation of previous physical culture trends. We know that *gymnasiums* began to emerge during the Roman Republic (509 BCE–27 BCE). The practices, specifically the exercise practices, found therein were inspired, if not outright taken, from Greek practices.

In his letters, Lucius Annaeus Seneca (4 BCE–CE 65) complained about the distractions of living over a gym,

> Beshrew me if I think anything more requisite than silence for a man who secludes himself in order to study! Imagine what a variety of noises reverberates about my ears!
>
> When your strenuous gentleman, for example, is exercising himself by flourishing leaden weights; when he is working hard, or else pretends to be working hard, I can hear him grunt; and whenever he releases his imprisoned breath, I can hear him panting in wheezy and high-pitched tones.[54]

Men were not the only ones exercising in gymnasiums. We have scant evidence of women's gymnastics cultures too. In Sicily there exists the *Villa Romana del Casale,* a fourth-century Roman villa which contains the 'bikini mosaic.' Found in the 'Room of Gymnasts' the mosaic shows several Roman women exercising with what appear to be dumbbells, small balls and perhaps a weighted medicine ball.[55]

Like the Ancient Greeks, the Romans appreciated the role diet and exercise played in maintaining health. Pliny the Elder, a Roman philosopher and statesman (23/24–79CE), wrote a great deal on weight loss and health. His writings paled, in comparison however, to the Roman physician Galen (129–c. 200/c. 216CE).

Galen wrote several books on diet, exercising with a small ball and exercise in general. His writings added an important medical component to the promotion of health and physical activity in general. Although he was not the first person to do so, Galen was an influential voice in the pursuit of 'exercise as medicine.'[56]

The gladiator training camps, *gymnasiums* and push for 'exercise as medicine' began to disappear with the fall of the Western Roman Empire from c. 376–476 CE. Political infighting, a succession of costly military defeats and the eventual collapse of the Roman military meant that the gymnasiums cultures of Greece and Rome was sidelined for several centuries. We will discuss this in greater detail in the next Chapter.

Conclusion

Surveying weightlifting and training in the Ancient World, a few key themes emerge. First that training has long held a considerable importance in a variety of human societies. This suggests that the need to train, lift, push and pull are closer to innate human behaviors than many would believe.

Secondly, we now know that training has always held a societal importance. It could, as was the case in Ancient India, be linked to military training, sport and even religious devotion. In China it could be linked to one's ancestors and one's own vitality. In

Ancient Greece, it meant these things and more. It meant the whole development of the self.

Finally, the weightlifting and exercise practices discussed here displayed the ingenuity behind individuals' exercise habits. People lifted heavy stones, rocks, rudimentary dumbbells, heavy clubs, and their own body weight to build muscle, strength and agility. Taken together it is clear that weightlifting not only existed in these ancient cultures, but it also thrived.

Key Themes from the Ancient World

- Physical training in the Ancient World was open to both men and women. Sources on women's physical culture are often, however, harder to find.

- How people trained in the Ancient World, the actual exercises they used, differed greatly. An exerciser in Athens trained differently to one in India. Likewise, with China and Egypt.

- Several of the motivations for training in the Ancient World are familiar to us even today. The need to lose weight, improve one's athletic ability, impress others and sustain one's health all underpinned certain exerciser's motivations.

- The Ancient World was also very different to the modern health climate. Strength, fitness and athleticism was also linked to funeral rites, honoring gods, and military training.

- The richness of these motivations came to influence later physical cultures.

CHAPTER 2

Disappearance and Re-Emergence

> *The majority of Christians believed that to participate in athletics or engage in physical training to glorify the body would contaminate the body, which 'housed' the soul, and would make the soul impure.*
>
> *The negative attitude that Medieval Christians had toward the body was in no small part the result of a reaction to paganism...*
>
> Robert A. Mechikoff & Steven Estes.[1]

It is strange to consider the relationship religion has with physical activity and gym cultures but, as Chapter One explained, religion often influenced how, why, and where people exercised. Mechikoff and Estes' quote gives a good description of physical culture during the 'Middle Ages' (500–1500 CE). It is not, as one can imagine, the entire story but it serves as a wonderful starting point. Physical activity and gym cultures thrived in the Ancient World. In Western Europe, the *gymnasium* cultures of Ancient Greece and Rome began to recede following the fall of the Western Roman Empire (c. 376–476 CE).

They almost disappeared but exercise, and its societal importance, nevertheless endured. The purpose of the current Chapter is to explain how and why exercise maintained its importance in the Western world across hundreds of years. More than that, we are going to track the relative disappearance, and vibrant recovery, of exercise during the Renaissance and

Enlightenment periods in Europe.

Doing this necessitates that we speak in generalizations. This is done to bring us from the pre-modern exercise cultures of the Ancient World to the tentative beginnings of the modern health climate in the eighteenth-century. To facilitate this journey, the Chapter will be divided into three distinct areas.

First, we will discuss physical culture in the Middle Ages (500–1500 CE). This was a time when the gymnasium cultures we found in Chapter One, disappeared. What replaced these cultures, and inadvertently maintained gymnasium cultures, will be explored. Here we will see the impact religion had in both suppressing and encouraging physical cultures as well as the role of military fighting in exercise systems.

The Middle Ages has been viewed by historians as a time when physical culture reached a low point. And yet, this low point did not endure. The Renaissance period (c. 1300–1550 CE) saw European countries rediscover Ancient Greek and Roman medical texts. This was a rediscovery of, and a falling in love with, physical culture once more. How, and where this rediscovery occurred will be discussed in the second section. For physical culturists it meant a mimicking of some of the same exercises, albeit for slightly different reasons, that exercisers in the Ancient World used.

Renaissance Europe rediscovered physical culture. Enlightenment Europe (c.1685–1815) advanced it. In the Enlightenment, European scholars, physicians, and educators held physical culture in a much higher esteem. Spurred on by their Renaissance predecessors, philosophers wrote about the need for sport and exercise. By the end of the eighteenth century, the discipline of physical training in schools was born. The introduction of physical training in schools marked a return to the gymnasium cultures of Ancient Greece (and in particular

Athens). Significantly, it also set the foundations for a much broader European, American (and later worldwide) interest in physical culture for all.

This Chapter looks once more at the motivations underpinning an individual, and a society's, interest in physical culture. It discusses who was included in the physical culture systems from this time and who was excluded. Similarly, it links physical culture to much broader socio-cultural events from these centuries. In all this, I encourage you to, once more, consider the societal meaning of the body and how the idea of an ideal body takes hold in societies over decades.

Physical Culture in the Middle Ages

The 'Middle Ages' or 'Dark Ages' as they were once referred to (500 CE–1500 CE) is typically depicted by historians as a time when sport and/or physical activities decreased in frequency.[2] This is not exactly true, as we shall see, but a fair assessment is that the gymnasium and physical culture communities of the Ancient World were oftentimes absent at this time.

Attempting to explain this downturn, several historians have cited the importance of the Catholic Church in Western Europe. In Ancient Athens, gymnasium cultures were linked to the overall development of the body/mind/spirit. To train the body was to improve the mind and vice versa. The body was thus a conduit to one's overall development.

Catholic doctrine during the 'Middle Ages' held a far more suspicious view of the body. The body was viewed as a 'vehicle of sin,' one which led people away from God and towards temptation.[3] While this doctrine was not all encompassing, it is important to stress the overall authority the Church held during this period.

In the vacuum created in Europe after the fall of the Roman Empire (c. 376–476), the Catholic Church became an important political actor. Clergymen ran schools, tended to the sick and advised political leaders. In France, religion was used to give legitimacy to the monarchs. According to French practices, the Capetian Kings (who ruled from 987 to 1792) claimed to be a mediator between God and the citizenry.

Society in the Middle-Ages can be crudely divided between the monarchs and aristocracy, the Church and then the peasant classes. The peasants toiled the fields and engaged in manual labor, while the nobility and upper classes were free to pursue sport, the arts and leisure.

Kings, and occasionally Queens, relied on the Catholic Church to give their rule legitimacy, to placate the citizenry and to act as moral arbitrators. This, in turn, gave the Church the ability to influence great swathes of European social life. Hence when historians say the Church viewed the body as a 'vehicle for sin,' this significantly impacted physical cultures.

Did this mean that sport and/or physical activity was non-existent during the Middle-Ages? Of course not. Early iterations of soccer existed (often taking part on religious holidays) while boxing and combat sports, alongside blood sports (like hunting, bull baiting, cock fighting, etc.) were popular. For the nobility, those of wealth and means, sports like colf and real tennis were played.[4]

Sport was still practiced during the Middle Ages. What of physical culture? Think back to the previous Chapter and our discussions of Ancient Sparta. As a warring society, Sparta used gymnastics, calisthenics, and combat sports to train children and men for the battlefield.

The warrior class of the Middle Age, 'knights,' exhibited a similar appreciation for physical culture. Knights typically came from the moneyed classes and exhibited a similar appreciation to the body as the Ancient Greeks. By the tenth century, the knight's system was formalized in several European countries.

The path to becoming a knight mimicked the system found in Ancient Sparta. Knights were trained in a system of ethics known as chivalry which related to manners, religion, and war. To become a knight, individuals had to train for up to fourteen years.[5]

Beginning at the age of eight, individuals were trained in gymnastics, calisthenics, horseback riding, fighting and much more. At this point it is worth commenting on the distinction between calisthenics and gymnastics. Following the work of Jan Todd, calisthenics is understood here as light, often rhythmic exercises done without implements.[6] Many dance teachers during this era were also callisthenic instructors. Gymnastics, on the other hand, is understood as more strenuous forms of exercise in which both the body and exercise implements are used.

Such training led to an incredibly fit cadre of willing fighters. There is also evidenced of knight 'strongmen' like Jean le Maingre or Boucicaut (c. 1366–1421 CE).

Many of the young aristocrats who followed this regimen became extremely athletic. Jean le Mainge, began life as a page at the court of Charles VI, and subsequently himself became Marshall of France.

French historian Jean Froissart later noted Boucicaut's incredible strength,

> he trained himself so well that at that time you couldn't find another gentleman in equal physical condition. He would do a somersault armed in all his armour except his bascinet, and dance armed in a mail shirt .... When he was at his lodgings, he would never cease to test himself with the other squires at throwing the lance or other tests of war.[7]

Boucicaut was unique in his appreciation for physical culture but the staples of a knight's regimen – horseback riding, fighting, jousting in heavy armor – meant that strength was a privileged component of a knight's training. Importantly, they were given plenty of opportunities to test their strength in battle.

Battles between, and within, European nations during the Middle Ages were common. Important for our purposes were the European Crusades (1095–1291 CE). The Crusades were a series of religious Wars between European and Islamic forces. The original intention of the Crusades was to 'liberate' Jerusalem from Islamic rule.

These wars were based on the notion that Jerusalem was an integral site of Christian worship. In 1095 Pope Urban II gave his official blessing for a European expedition to place Jerusalem under Catholic rulers. Urban's support for this project had two significant ramifications. It initiated a series of wars between European and Islamic forces and gave a religious blessing to those who fought.[8]

Catholic doctrine adhered to the idea of 'thou shalt not kill.' The Crusades was an obvious exception. In essence, Urban gave European knights a religious endorsement to fight. This gave the knightly training school a legitimacy which helped sustained its practices. Knights training for battle were engaged then in a religious war.

As was the case in the Ancient World, we have some scant evidence of women participating in the fighting, especially in the eleventh and twelfth century. Sophie Harwood's research on medieval women noted Islamic writings from this period which commented on the 'large numbers of Christian women' who participated in fighting. This seems to have dwindled in later centuries.

Some women were later accepted into military orders like the Knights Templar, Knights Hospitaller and the Teutonic Order although it is very difficult to say whether these women were trained using the same chivalric system as men.[9]

Returning to our 'body as a vehicle of sin' idea, knights were excluded. Likewise, this gave a certain respectability to medieval tournaments between knights where contestants engaged in sword-fighting, horseback riding and jousting. Physical culture in gymnasiums did not exist but physical activities and the act of training the body certainly did.

The multiple Crusades into the Middle East rarely succeeded in their goals, or in sustaining their goals. What they did succeed in was causing a huge amount of geo-political division and disasters. An unintended consequence of this was the spread of knowledge from the Middle East into Europe.

When European armies traversed across the Silk Road (the network of trade routes between the Middle East and Asia), they were exposed to ideas and practices previously unknown. When the instabilities caused by the Crusades resulted in the fall of Constantinople in 1453, large numbers of scholars migrated to mainland Europe. They brought texts and manuscripts from Ancient Greece which, in turn, helped Europeans to 'rediscover' old Greco-Roan practices.[10]

Rediscovering Physical Culture in the Renaissance

Although several later battles were labelled Crusades, historians generally cite 1291 as the end of the original Crusade campaign.[11] This marked the tentative end of the Middle Ages (although it ended at different points in different countries) and the beginning of the Renaissance in mainland Europe. Invigorated by the rediscovery of ancient materials from the modern world, European societies began a period of 'cultural rebirth.'

The Catholic Church still held political and social importance, but it had to compete with new work and philosophies. Traditionally the Renaissance period was depicted as a total break from the Medieval Period, but many know see it as a period of gradual change.[12]

Underpinning the 'Renaissance ethos' was the philosophy of humanism which, broadly speaking meant an appreciation for the humanities – literature, art, poetry, history, etc. This was not an areligious movement, but rather an attempt to 'purify' Christianity through the melding together of devotion and prolonged study.

The Renaissance began in mainland Europe, especially modern-day Italy, and spread across the continent. Within this new approach to life was a new approach to the physical body. Humanist philosophies did not view the body as a 'vehicle of sin' but rather as an object of enquiry.

It was no longer something to be avoided or ignored but something to be placed under intense scrutiny. While the medical practices this brought forth are a different topic for a different book, the Renaissance period saw an uptick in sport and physical culture practices across fourteenth and fifteenth century Europe.

Robert Mechikoff and Steven Estes explained it elegantly as follows,

> This philosophy, known as humanism, emphasised our 'humanness' rather than our spiritual selves. As a direct consequence of this type of thinking, affairs of the human body were considered much more acceptable. Sport and physical education were direct beneficiaries of this type of thought.[13]

But what, you're no doubt wondering, did this mean for exercising? It meant a growth in educational, medical, and recreational physical cultures, all of which took inspiration from Greco-Roman texts. We have, for example, evidence of physical education emerging during this period in the form of Vittorino da Feltre (1378–1446), an Italian humanist, philosopher, and educator.

Inspired by Plato, and the educational models of Ancient Sparta, da Feltre opened a school in Mantua, Italy, called *La Casa Giocosa* (The House of Joy) where he trained young noblemen and women. Although the number of girls attending his school is thought to be low, their existence highlighted da Feltre's humanist belief in exercise for all. Each day students were engaged with two or more hours exercise a day in the form of leaping, riding, fencing, gymnastics and much more.[14]

While physical education did not become a hugely popular idea until the Enlightenment Period, da Feltre's early experiments had supporters in Italy. It marked a return to the Greco-Roman idea of a healthy mind and a healthy body working together in unison. Physical education was tentatively emerging in schools but who were the students?

Schools and universities were the preserve of two distinct groups in the Renaissance period. Higher learning was open to those seeking entrance into the Church as a priest, and the children of wealthy families. Physical educationalists like da Feltre, and his supporters, trained wealthy children. This is not the only time we will be confronted with the idea that money impacted one's ability to engage in physical culture.

In Ancient Rome physicians like Galen (129–c. 216) recommended some forms of mild physical activity to cure several minor diseases and complaints. One of the first Renaissance authors to revive this idea was Petrarch (1304–1374) whose wonderfully titled *Invectives against a Physician* pamphlet argued that exercise could be used to treat disease. Petrarch's four-part pamphlet series against physicians and modern medicine may have been motivated by his disdain for doctors, but his argument in favor of exercise was significant.[15]

A large number of Renaissance writers following in Petrarch's wake continued with the idea that moderation, exercise and good diet could protect the body against diseases. Inspiring such individuals were Ancient Greek physicians like Hippocrates – of Hippocratic oath importance – (c. 460–c. 370 BCE) and the Roman physician Galen.

One such example is Regimen sanitatis Salernitanum published in 1480 by a medieval medical school in southern Italy. Inspired by Galen's writings, it helped bring more familiarity with Roman thought on medical gymnastics and exercise to Italian readers.

Where initially a great deal of medical writings were created for the educated (religious or monied) classes, works were eventually created for the general public. In 1536 Thomas Elyot (1490–1546) published *Castel of Helthe* with a simple aim in mind. Elyot wanted to create a manual for poorer classes on how to maintain their health.

Roy Shepard cited the *Castel of Helthe* as an influential health text both in terms of making self-care possible and raising awareness of physical cultures.[16] Elyot's book, which underwent fifteen re-editions by 1610, included notes on walking, exercising with a heavy object and a number of other movements designed to strengthen and enrich the body.

Before moving from the Renaissance, there are two books and authors that need to be mentioned for their sheer popularity. One helped to link one's health to their religious devotion while the other is perhaps most famous for its remarkable depictions of Greco-Roman exercise in the gymnasium.

In the previous section we noted the Catholic tendency to view the body as a 'vehicle of sin.' In 1558 an Italian nobleman named Luigi Cornaro published *The Sure and Certain Method of Attaining a Long and Healthful Life* which argued that God 'willed' longevity in humans. It was thus not immoral to focus on one's body, but rather a spiritual pathway.[17]

Cornaro's health writings (of which there were four popular works) were biblical in their content. Readers were told that Cornaro had spent the first half of his life living a sinful existence defined by drinking, eating and socializing too much. At the age of thirty-five he realized his health was failing him and, after a visit to the doctor, decided to entirely reform his ways.

From then, Cornaro ate a sparse diet, taking only twelve ounces of food and fourteen ounces of new wine divided across four meals. Despite the reservations of his friends and family this low quantity of food, Cornaro returned to full health. In fact, he told readers that he had never felt better.

It is said that Cornaro died in his late eighties, nineties or, in some cases, after he passed one hundred years old. What is important is that Cornaro claimed that his diet helped make him a calmer, more empathetic and happier person. His diet had moved him from sinning to spirituality.

His pamphlets, much like Thomas Elyot's *Castel of Helthe* went through multiple re-editions and challenged the idea of the body as a 'vehicle for sin.' In line with broader Renaissance thinkers, the body was an object in need of cultivation.

The Cornaro Story?

Luigi Cornaro's pamphlets claimed that his reckless ways caused him a great deal of ill health. Seeking to improve his health and life, Cornaro discovered

> an unorthodox way of eating which helped revive his body. While friends and family told him not to do it, he was convinced in his methods. He later shared this information so that others could benefit.
>
> While this sort of diet 'redemption' story was rarer in Cornaro's time, they are commonplace today. Can you think of similar 'redemption' stories with diets like the Paleo, Keto, 5/2, Intermittent Fasting or Carnivore diets? What about those who promote juices, raw food or other restrictive diets?
>
> Typically, we are told that a particular diet, food or supplement can reform our lives. Why are these stories so powerful?

Cornaro promoted restrictive diets. Others vigorous activity. In 1569 Italian physician Hieronymus Mercuriale published *De Arte Gymnastica Aput Ancientes* (Art of Gymnastics Among the Ancients). Using the writings of more than ninety other authors (ancient and modern) Mercuriale's book was one of the most important exercise tracts of its time.

Historians have credited Mercuriale with helping to re-ignite the European interest in gymnasium cultures.[18] Why was Mercuriale so influential? Especially given that *De Arte Gymnastica* was largely a collection of other people's ideas and writings? Part of its popularity had to do with the illustrations it contained.

What do you notice about the illustration in Figure 2.1?

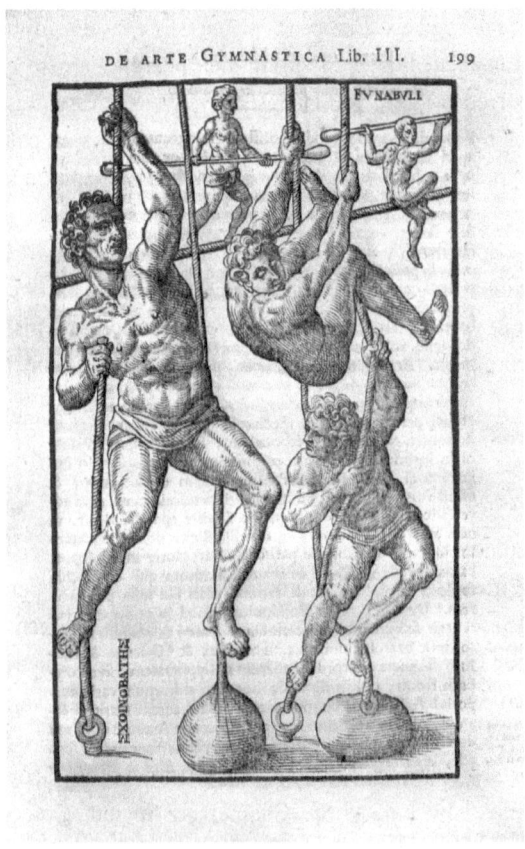

Figure 2.1. Mercuriale, 'De Arte Gymnastica,' 1672.[19]

Specifically, what kinds of bodies do you see? Are they lean and slim or muscular and powerful? Mercuriale's book was important for two reasons. It distilled a great deal of information into a highly readable text and showcased illustrations of strong and powerful male bodies.

The illustrations in Mercuriale's book came at a time when

European artists were mimicking old Greco-Roman sculptures of muscular bodies. European planners were also discovering actual Roman sculptures of strong men like the Farnese Hercules (rediscovered in 1546). This interest in overt strength and muscularity bode well for the following century's interest in physical culture.

As a final note, it is important to recognize the three kinds of physical culture Mercuriale recognized - *gymnastica medica* (exercise to enhance health), *gymnastica bellica* (sport used as preparation for war) and *gymnastica atletica* (what we would class as physical culture and/or exercise for sport). This nuance in describing exercise intensified during the Enlightenment.

Exercise in the Enlightenment

The Renaissance witnessed the rediscovery of Greco-Roman training ideals, but the Enlightenment (roughly the period between 1685 and 1815) saw an increased attention given over to training in daily life. This took form in many different areas but, before going into that, we need to briefly discuss the general tenets of Enlightenment philosophy.

It may seem strange to begin a discussion on physical culture with philosophy but, as the Chapter on Ancient Greece made clear that philosophy and physical training have a long history. The Enlightenment was a period when philosophers like John Locke (1632–1704), Isaac Newton (1643–1706), Voltaire (1694–1778), Benjamin Franklin, (1706–1790), Frederick the Great (1712–1786), Jean-Jacques Rousseau (1712–1778), Denis Diderot (1713–1784), Thomas Paine (1737–1809) and Mary Wollstonecraft (1759–1797) questioned old ideals and sought to find new answers through logic.

It would be ambitious, and wrong, to define an 'Enlightenment philosophy, given that thinkers from these areas examined everything from the very structure of government and civilization to the theory of gravity. What we can do, however, is say that this period was defined by an attempt to logically understand the Universe.

Importantly, for us, many of these influential philosophers had been inspired by the Renaissance period's welcoming of sport and physical culture. During the Enlightenment many of these individuals began to write about the necessity of physical culture for men and women.

In *A Vindication of the Rights of Women* (1792), Wollstonecraft rallied against the educational and societal inequities facing women. On the subject of exercise Wollstonecraft wrote that,

> I wish to persuade women to endeavor to acquire strength, both of mind and body. Let us then by being allowed to take the same exercises as boys, not only during infancy, but youth, arrive at perfection of the body, that we may know how far the natural superiority of man.[20]

As Jan Todd noted in an encompassing work on American physical culture, Wollstonecraft's arguments proved very influential for some in the nineteenth century.[21] *A Vindication of the Rights of Women* was the impetus for many in the expansion of physical and intellectual education for women. One of the early founders of the suffrage movement in America, Elizabeth Cady Stanton, wrote in 1851 about the need for equality between men and women's exercise.

For Todd, Wollstonecraft was part of an intellectual movement daring to produce a form of 'majestic womanhood' that was strong in body and mind. Adherents included Wollstonecraft, physician educator Dio Lewis (1823–1886), phrenologist Orson Fowler

(1809–1887), and Elizabeth Blackwell (1821–1910) among others.[22]

Rousseau's 1762 work *Emile, or On Education* became a classical Enlightenment endorsement of physical culture. The novel, as the next Chapter will discuss, served as motivation for many physical trainers in the nineteenth century.

Without going into too much detail, Rousseau's novel was Athenian in its outlook on an education system that trained mind and body. He focused on the holism between mind and body. Accordingly, Emile contained passages like,

> The body must needs be vigorous in order to obey the soul a good servant ought to be robust ... The weaker the body, the more it commands; the stronger it is, the better it obeys.

And,

> In order to make him wise and reasonable; let him work, and move about, and run, and shout, and be continually in motion; let him be a man in vigor, and soon he will be such by force of reason.[23]

While Wollstonecraft and Rousseau both wrote of the need for women's exercise, they differed in its application. Using the fictious character Sophie, Rousseau argued that women should not try to be strong and fit like boys but rather they should exercise to become more attractive to men and therefore birth healthier children.[24]

Enlightenment writers clearly appreciated physical training and exercise, but what about others? The eighteenth century laid the foundation for a great deal of exercise in the following century. This was true across medical, recreational, and educational fields. One such example of this came in 1705 when English physician Francis

Fuller (1670–1706) published *Medicina Gymnastica: or a Treatise Concerning the Power of Exercise with Respect to the Animal.*

Written to discuss the variety of ways in which exercise or movement benefitted the body, Fuller's work was just one of many published by British doctors during this period. Fuller was joined by other physicians like George Cheyne, Thomas Sydenham and James Mackenzie, all of whom wrote on the value of physical activity when it came to overall health.[25] The idea of exercise as medicine was slowly becoming established.

Importantly these messages were becoming global in their appeal. Fuller's book on medicine and gymnastics was translated into several European languages, as were several of his colleagues' works. British doctors were reading health tracts written in mainland Europe and vice-versa. This globalization of health material, which began in the Renaissance, intensified.

The Enlightenment period also witnessed the growth of individual strongmen and strongwomen acts. Famous eighteenth century English strongman Thomas Topham (c. 1710–1749) is a wonderful example of this. When he became the landlord of a pub in London, Topham realized that he could put his strength to good measure.

Using his tavern as a base, Topham put on audacious displays of strength which ranged from rolling up pewter plates to bending an iron fireplace poker. He was also known to sit on the ground with his feet propped against a wall or stump. From there he would hold back horses who had been urged to go forward.[26]

As an insight into Topham's strength, the History Channel commissioned a show in 2019 in which modern competitors from the World Strongest Man contest recreated historical lifts. While one of the strongmen, (Brian Shaw, 1982–) ultimately defeated Topham's 1836 lbs. record with a 2,028 lbs. lift, they all conceded to Topham's immense strength, which came at a time before modern gyms, nutrition or anabolic steroids.[27]

Topham became a *cause célèbre* for Enlightenment thinkers. British philosopher, clergyman, and engineer John Theophilus Desaguliers brought Topham to the attention of the Royal Society of London where Desaguliers and others began to scientifically study Topham's feats of strength, as well as other strong men. Desaguliers even wrote about Topham's physiological advantages in his 1734 work *A Course Of Experimental Philosophy*.[28]

Desaguliers' interactions with Topham reflected the scientific enquiry which underpinned the Enlightenment. People were fascinated by the mystery of life and wanted to impose order and rationality upon it. This did not mean, however, that romantic or creative ideals did not also have their importance.

John-Jacque Rousseau's work *Emile* helped inspire dozens of educators to trial physical education and gymnastics in their schools. Equally important, however, was the 'rediscovery' of Grecian sculpture and architecture in the late eighteenth and early nineteenth century. For Western eyes a particularly critical example of this was the display of the Elgin Marbles in London in 1807.

The display intensified an interest in Greco-Roman culture, education and, importantly, exercise. For many individuals, ancient Grecian statues became the prime example of what bodily perfection was.[29] So too did an increasing interest in measuring the body but we will come back to this point in the next Chapter.

Take, for example, the mid-nineteenth-century English gymnast, George Forrest who said of his own generation,

> We English, possess perhaps the finest and strongest figures of all European nations ...We ... are apparently devoid of that beautiful series of muscles that run round the entire waist, and show to such advantage in the ancient statues.[30]

It is also telling that physical culturists from the late nineteenth and early twentieth century would take photographs of themselves recreating the poses of Greek statues for the very simple reason that this was the biggest point of comparison for individuals.

Perhaps the most important individual inspired by Rousseau and the growing interest in Greco-Roman statuary was undoubtedly German educator and writer Johann Bernhard Basedow (1723-1790). During this period Basedow became a devout proponent of physical education.

In 1774 Basedow published *Das Ekmentarwerk,* a four-volume book dedicated to a simple and singular goal – how best to educate young men. The book helped shape the minds of many of the later physical educators discussed in Chapter Three.

For now it is important to note that *Das Ekmentarwerk* was published at the same time that Basedow opened his own school in Dessau, Germany called the *Philanthropinum*. The *Philanthropinum* became the place where Basedow's dreams came to fruition. His early prospectus split the school day between study, recreation and manual labor.

What we will pay attention to here is not Basedow's novel approach to education, although it fascinated many contemporaries. Instead we will discuss the instructors he hired and the people he inspired. From the late 1770s, Basedow's *Philanthropinum* became one of the most attractive places to work for men interested in physical education.

His first recreational and gymnastics instructor, Johann Friedrich Simon, brought 'Greek Gymnastics' to the school. His successor, Johann Jacob Du Toit, brought swimming, skating, marches and other grueling activities. Soon others copied both Basedow's philosophy, and the exercises used by his instructors. One such individual was Christian Gottliff Salzmann (1744-

1811), who founded his own *Philanthropinum* at Schnepfenthal, near Gotha.[31]

Salzmann's school inadvertently created a historical lineage. Salzmann's physical training instructor for over thirteen years was Johann Friedrich GutsMuths (1759-1839). Following a physical training curriculum like that found in Basedow's school, GutsMuths continued to refine his teachings and his ideas.

In 1793, GutsMuths published a huge two volume tome entitled *Gymnastik für die Jugend* (or *Gymnastics for Children*). Despite its relatively banal title, GutsMuth's book was a forceful rallying call for strenuous activity and manliness.

To spare you the several hundred page read, GutsMuth argued that the current generation of young men were too weak in body and mind. Prescribing an exercise regimen of up to ten hours exercise a week, GutsMuth ascribed to create an 'ideal man' who could become the ideal warrior for the State.

GutsMuth took the ideas of Basedow, Rousseau and others, contributed his own ideas and married them with a rising nationalist sentiment. In effect, he linked physical culture to the military. This intensified the popularity of physical culture across Europe in the nineteenth century. Soon other GutsMuth inspired trainers emerged with fascinating results.

Conclusion

The re-appearance and intensification of physical culture in Western society was not an easy or coherent process. There was no 'Big Bang' moment in the rediscovery of physical culture, but rather multiple occurrences happening simultaneously.

Here we discussed the 'disappearance' of physical culture during the Middle Ages and the linkage between the military and physical cultures. Physical training was still appreciated during this period, but more for fighting, than educational, purposes.

During the Renaissance period, Western Europe began to assimilate older Greco-Roman ideas into medicine, educational and recreational patterns. The European appreciation for Greco-Roman culture during this period helped to rid societies of the idea that training the body was a sinful process and instead an act of rationalism and holistic development.

The Enlightenment helped solidify these ideas into Western thought. During his epoch physical culture was formally brought into classrooms across Europe. Philosophers noted the importance of training the body for mind and body (what a Greek idea!) and educators introduced training to children. We also saw the sporadic emergence of those strength performers who would drive physical culture's popularity in the following century.

Key Themes from the Disappearance and Re-Emergence

- Physical training in the Middle Ages was predominately linked to fighting and the Knightly Arts like fencing. Owing to religious doctrine training the body was viewed suspiciously. It needed to be linked to military endeavors. Hence, Knights became the physical culturists of the age.
- While the Middle Ages saw a lessening of physical culture's popularity, it grew in the following era, the Renaissance, and became solidified during the Enlightenment.
- During the Renaissance, physical culture was once more discussed in military, educational and medical fields.
- The desire for rationality during the Enlightenment produced the first modern efforts to scientifically study physical culture. This period also produced philosophical reasoning for the importance of physical culture in classrooms.
- Physical culture, as a modern phenomenon, grew exponentially in the nineteenth century. This was due, in part, to greater accessibility to contemporary and ancient writings and cultures.

CHAPTER 3

The Birth of Physical Culture

> *Twenty years ago, the term Physical Culture was scarcely known. Nowadays, everyone understands its meaning...*
>
> A. Wallace, 1908.[1]

Why was Wallace, a writer for the English fitness publication *Health and Strength,* so confident that people knew what physical culture was when he wrote the above sentence in 1908 and, more importantly, was he correct?

Cast your mind back to the Introduction where we discussed the various definitions of physical culture. One of those definitions referred to the so-called 'physical culture movement.' This was a time between the late 1800s and early 1900s when people began to refer to weightlifting, physical activity and monitoring their diets as physical culture.

Wallace was correct in citing the growing popularity of physical culture. He might have been a tad ambitious, but he was correct. From the early nineteenth century gymnasium cultures grew exponentially in popularity across Europe and the United States.

When Wallace's book was published, physical culture in gyms, classrooms, military barracks, and homes was commonplace. Early bodybuilding shows existed, weightlifting was a competitive sport and gym equipment was more varied. During the first half of the twentieth century these processes were defined to a remarkable degree.

In the last Chapter we focused on hundreds of years of human history. Here we will be focusing on a much shorter period – the early 1800s to the 1930s. This Chapter is all about the intensification of physical culture.

Section One examines the growth of physical culture in the first half of the nineteenth century. Specifically, we will discuss the rise of new military and recreational physical cultures. This was a time when fitness truly became globalized, when exercise practices found in India emerged in England, when those used in Germany, moved to America and so on.

Section Two discusses the physical culture movement that Wallace referred to. That is, physical culture from the 1890s to the 1920s. This period will look remarkably modern to you. There will be bodybuilding shows, supplements, workout books, and weightlifting contests.

Finally, we will explore physical culture in the period between World War One (1914-1918) and the Second World War (1939-1945). The 'interwar period' saw governments begin to promote physical culture for their citizens. Here, physical culture became a method of training future soldiers, of alleviating burdens on health systems and of reinforcing racial hierarchies.

Wallace was right. Physical culture, as a term and as a lifestyle, was popularized during his period. It reached, and even perhaps surpassed, the appreciation shown by the Ancient Greeks for exercise. It became a part of everyday life and a tool for governments the world over. This physical culture movement set the origins for our modern environment.

The Rise of Gymnastics

> *The astonishing development of popular interest in gymnastics which has taken place in Germany and other European countries can be traced directly to Jahn's work ...* [2]

Fred Eugene Leonard, 1923.

Fred Eugene Leonard was one of the first individuals to chronicle the history of physical education. He helped to historicize some of the early teachers of gymnastics in the nineteenth century and, in essence, provided a great starting point for later historians.

Now that you know who Leonard is, you are probably wondering about Jahn. Jahn was a Prussian gymnast whose branch of nationalist gymnastics became a worldwide phenomenon. Friedrich Ludwig Jahn (1778–1852 CE) was born in Lanz, Brandenburg, in 1778. Crucially, his formative years, at university, came at a time of great political instability in Europe.

In 1789 the French Revolution began, which sent shockwaves around Europe. Inspired, in part, by the political philosophies of John-Jacque Rousseau – the man studied in the last Chapter – the Revolution was fueled by a desire to open voting rights in France, to restructure the economy and to address institutional corruptions.

Now the Revolution doesn't necessarily contribute to the history of physical culture save in one important way – it produced Napoléon Bonaparte.

Napoléon (1769–1821), led several of France's armies during the Revolution and became Emperor of France from 1804-1814 and again, briefly, in 1815. Leading France from the chaos of the Revolution, Napoléon expanded France's borders across Europe.

This included Jahn's own homeland – what we would now call Germany.

As a university student, Jahn fought, and lost, against Napoleon's armies at Jena and Auerstedt (1806). Napoléon's soldiers exuded physical fitness. They were filled with young men, capable of covering vast distances in a short period of time and could quickly move around the battlefield.[3]

Jahn became convinced that the only way to safeguard Germany's borders in future was to make German men stronger and fitter than their enemies. One of his many books, *Deutsches Volkstum* (The German Way of Life), written in 1810, explained it thusly,

> Only when all men of military age have become capable through physical education of bearing arms, have become ready for combat through weapon training, prompt to strike … can a people be called militarily prepared.[4]

In 1809, Jahn began teaching at the Graue Kloster school, a high school in Berlin. While there, Jahn began playing games with students outside Halle at the Hasenhide park. Within a year 80 men and boys began to train at a rudimentary outdoor gymnasium at Hasenhide.[5] Three years later numbers rose to five hundred and, by 1817, roughly a thousand men trained there.

There they trained using callisthenic exercises and equipment (which at the time meant balancing beams and climbing frames). For Jahn he wanted to make stronger men while simultaneously increasing their *Deutschheit* (or Germanness).[6] If it is not clear, Jahn was a deeply political person with outspoken views. Problematically for Jahn, he did not confine his views to the gymnasium.

In 1817 he publicly led a ceremonial burning of 'reactionary books.' His gymnasiums increasingly turned into places for political discussions. This worried authorities in Berlin, who feared Jahn's growing strength. He was arrested in 1819 and placed under house arrest. Eventually he was told to leave Berlin and never return while his training sites were closed.

Around this time, a generation of Jahn inspired gymnasts migrated across the world, bringing his system with him. Importantly, Jahn returned to Berlin in 1840 and was elected to parliament in 1848. That same year revolutions erupted across Europe. In Prussia, many *Turner* members joined in demands for greater political freedoms but with little success.

The revolution failed and the *Turnverein* were closed once more. This time, thousands of Turners emigrated from Germany. Many went to the United States and Canada, where they brought Jahn's system with them, albeit oftentimes without its nationalist undertones.[7] By the late nineteenth century it should also be noted that many *Turnverein* clubs were open to men and women.[8]

Jahn's system became a global phenomenon and was used for the next several decades in schools, militaries and gymnasiums in Europe (we will turn to the United States shortly). His was not the only system to receive renown. Competing with Jahn's system of gymnastics was the Swedish or Ling gymnastics system created by Pehr Henrik Ling (1776–1839CE).

Ling/Swedish gymnastics (the terms were used interchangeably during the nineteenth and early twentieth century) differed from Jahn's system practically and philosophically. The exercises employed by Ling were gentler, open to both sexes and premised on Ling's idea that exercise could serve as a form of massage and medical treatment.[9]

This differing philosophy stemmed from Ling's different life-path. Where Jahn fought in the Napoleonic Wars, Ling studied theology at Uppsala University in Sweden. Where Jahn was concerned with masculinity and nationalism, Ling worried about ill health and pain. Finally, where Jahn was a believer in tough and vigorous activity, Ling stressed balance, coordination, and control.

Ling's system spread from Sweden around Europe, Asia, and later America. Unlike Jahn, whose system was exported, in part, thanks to the banishment of members from Germany, Ling's system spread through the books of his admirers, as well as word of mouth.[10] Other systems did exist, most notably the Sokol system of physical culture from Prague (founded 1862), but the nineteenth century was largely defined by Swedish or Turner gymnastics.[11]

Jahn's system was staunchly nationalist at that. Ling, on the other hand, recognized the value physical culture had for both sexes and, in turn, advised its usage by men and women. While women's exercise still suffered from male prejudices around the female body, Ling's system helped, tentatively, to revise some ideas about women's exercise.

The Global Workout?

Do you ever reflect on the kinds of exercises you do in the gym? Thanks to globalization, and the popularity of sports like bodybuilding, weightlifting and powerlifting, the exercises trainees do around the world have become remarkably similar.[12]

Think back to the exercises discussed in our Chapter on the Ancient World. How people trained in Ancient Athens was different to Egypt and was different to India. Nowadays thanks to online media, sport and

The Birth of Physical Culture

> commerce, individuals who train in the United States use the same exercises are those in Great Britain and those in India or China. We even have gym chains becoming worldwide phenomena.
>
> For want of a better phrase, we are now all global exercisers! And this process began during the nineteenth century with Jahn, Ling and others.

Away from Jahn or Ling there were people like Phokion Heinrich Clias (1782-1854CE) who taught gymnastics in England, France and Switzerland, Monsieur J.A. Beaujeu (c. 1780-1832CE) who taught gymnastics in Liverpool and Dublin or Don Francisco Amorós y Ondeano (1770–1848CE) who was an instructor in France and Spain.[13] These trainers regularly cited other European writers like GutsMuth, Jahn or Ling in their works and, in turn, brought greater attention to these systems.

European ideas, and teachers, did make their mark in the United States. German emigres, and their *Turner* system, came in the 1820s. Charles Beck (1798-1866) taught Latin and gymnastics at the Round Hill School from 1825, Karl Follen (1796–1840) taught German at Harvard University and helped established gymnastics there. Likewise, Franz Lieber (1798–1872), opened a public gym in Boston Commons.[14] Likewise, Jan Todd has found evidence that Madame Beaujeu, the wife of Dublin based trainer Monsieur Beaujeu, likely travelled to the United States in 1841 where she operated a gym as Ms. Hawley.[15]

European influence notwithstanding, two of the most influential American trainers in the mid-nineteenth century were American educators Catharine Beecher (1800-1878) and Diocletian 'Dio'

Lewis (1823–1886). An influential educator and writer, Beecher introduced light calisthenics for girls into her schools as early as 1827.[16] Beecher eventually published two books for women – *Letters to the People on Health and Happiness* (1855) and *Physiology and Calisthenics* (1856).[17]

Beecher's exercise system, which was used to great effect in many American schools, was defined by its gentleness relative to men's physical education. Lewis, on the other hand, proved a devout believer in the need for strenuous exercise. He was a temperance leader, a trained doctor who promoted homoeopathy and was the founder of a Physical Training institute in 1861.[18]

In 1862 Lewis published a training manual entitled *The New Gymnastics for Men, Women and Children* which opened with the wonderful line 'like air and food, these exercises are adapted to both sexes, and to persons of all ages.' Using a combination of his own training theories, and those translated from European texts, Lewis offered readers a training system comprised of dumbbells, club swinging, gymnastics, bean bag throwing and, even wrestling.

It was truly groundbreaking and was arguably one of the most strenuous exercise systems created for girls at this time.[19] Lewis' writings were highly praised by educators and those in the United States who believed that strenuous physical education for men and women would ensure healthier generations in the future.[20] Importantly, Lewis' books were also warmly received by some in Britain as well.[21]

This globalization wasn't confined to ideas, it also extended to objects. In 1824 Henry Torrens, Adjunct General to the Forces in the British military recommended the use of a wooden club in order to 'supple the recruit ... open his chest and give freedom to the muscles.'[22] This wooden club was, in fact, inspired by the Indian clubs discussed in Chapter One.

Indian club swinging – the swinging of small wooden clubs – became one of the first major fitness fads of the nineteenth century. From Britain, these clubs spread to Europe, the United States and, in time, the colonial world. Importantly they were used by men and women, albeit with the caveat that men were encouraged to lift heavy clubs, and women light clubs.

The British military was responsible for bringing Indian club swinging from India to Europe. It was also responsible for creating one of the first formalized military training systems. In 1860, the British military created a training system which would be used throughout the British Empire (which held 400 million people by 1914).

From 1853 to 1856, the British fought in the Crimean War. The casualty rates they incurred, often due to poor hygiene, caused military thinkers to revise the military's health and training programmes. Thus in the late 1850s, a Scottish physical educationalist named Archibald Maclaren was asked to create a training programme for troops.

Knowledgeable in European and British training methods, Maclaren's programme combined the callisthenic exercises of Jahn and Ling with Indian club swinging and dumbbell lifting. Maclaren's system was used by the British military until the early 1900s and was used by hundreds of thousands of men around the world.[23]

Before we move on to the true 'birth' of physical culture, there's a pressing issue that needs to be explored – is physical culture dangerous? Your natural response might be to ask for who? Despite individuals like Beecher, Lewis, and countless others who promoted some form of physical activity for women, a common argument during this century was that exercise, or excessive exercise, was dangerous for the female body.

Sport historian Martha Verbrugge has previously cited a 'cult of female frailty' in the nineteenth century to refer to a strongly held societal belief that women's bodies were unable to endure physical hardship.[24] This idea permeated certain educational, medical, and philosophical discourses.

Particularly important in promoting this idea were medical experts who cited the menstrual cycle and the ability to give birth as two reasons why women's bodies were inherently less than men's bodies.[25] Acting as social leaders, physicians influenced the practices of physical culture instructors who – based on flawed medical opinion – promoted less intense exercise for women.

This was a practice rooted in broader gender inequalities of the age and, as Roberta Park's research demonstrated, was a very attractive way of thinking for many in the United States.[26] In Britain an obvious example of this way of thinking can be found in the use of Indian clubs.

In 1834, Donald Walker published *British Manly Exercise,* one of the century's most popular sport and exercise books. Two years later Walker published *Exercises for Ladies Designed to Preserve and Improve their Beauty.* Where Walker prescribed Indian club swinging for men, he promoted an Indian sceptre – which was smaller and more ornamental - for women. The sceptres were lighter than the clubs Walker promoted for men and thus deemed more 'appropriate' for women's delicate frames.[27]

Medical discourses drove the idea that physical culture could be damaging for women – although as we have seen not everyone agreed with this statement. There was also a great deal of medical confusion around whether or not heavy weight training was beneficial.

One proponent of heavy weightlifting was George Barker Windship (1834–1876CE), a Harvard trained doctor who became a convert to heavy weight training. Windship first undertook gymnastics during his undergraduate days at Harvard, where he

The Birth of Physical Culture

studied medicine. Windship's motivation at the time was simple – he wanted to improve his strength and stature.

He was sixteen years old when he enrolled in Harvard and weighed less than one hundred pounds. In time he became known as the strongest man in Harvard. On a trip to Rochester, New York, in 1854, Windship encountered a 'lifting machine' on the street. This 'lifting machine,' as Jan Todd's biography of Windship explained, resembled a partial deadlift or a hand and thigh lift.

In any case, Windship managed to lift 420 lbs. but, this did not impress the assembled spectators. Curious about improving his strength, Windship returned to Boston, and devised his own 'lifting machine' in his backyard. In time he could lift 2,600 lbs. on the 'health lift' – the name eventually given to this kind of machine.

Touring the East Coast of the United States, Windship gave public lectures during which he lifted hundreds of pounds on the Health Lift. Significantly, he argued that men and women should do likewise to improve their health. Exercise was becoming more and more popular during this period (the 1860s/70s) but very few people recommended heavy weight training. Many doctors feared that heavy weightlifting would strain the heart and tax the body.

The public initially ignored these criticisms. Windship ran a gym in Boston, and others, like George Butler, opened their own health lift studios, some of which were open to women. In 1876 tragedy struck Windship. He died of a stroke aged forty-two.[28] Although Windship was a trained doctor, many took his early demise as proof that heavy weightlifting was dangerous. Debates about whether heavy weightlifting was dangerous lasted for several more decades.

The 'Birth' of Physical Culture

Commenting briefly on the use of the term physical culture, Jan Todd traced its origins to Adolphus Vongnieur's 1787 book *A Treatise on the Bane of Vice* to describe growth and maturation. By the mid-nineteenth century the term showed up in the writings of individuals previously discussed here like Dio Lewis. By the end of the nineteenth century, physical culture was used to describe physical education and physical training.

In the United States and Britain, the term physical culture began to fall out of favor in the 1920s and 1930s – to be replaced by other names like weightlifting, physical education, etc., although the physical culture is still used in many parts of Europe to describe physical education.[29]

Physical culture, as a term, grew in popularity, and was used around the world, during the course of the nineteenth century, especially in its latter decades. Explaining how and why this happened necessitates a journey to mainland Europe in the late 1880s.

There that we find a young Prussian strongman, Friedrich Wilhelm Müller (1867–1925CE), soon to be known as Eugen Sandow. At that time Müller was a travelling strength performer and wrestler who worked in the gymnasium of fellow strength athlete Ludwig Durlacher ('Louis Attila').

Impressed with Müller's raw athleticism, Durlarcher set about mentoring the strongman. They travelled around Europe, performed feats of strength and, where possible, engaged in audacious public stunts.

One such stunt came in 1889 when Durlarcher became aware of a London based strongman, Charles 'Samson' Sampson, who issued strength challenges to his audience during shows. If anyone could defeat Samson, they won a cash prize and the title of 'World's Strongest Man.'

Travelling to London with Durlarcher, Müller accepted Samson's challenge and, over the course of two nights, defeated Samson and his sidekick Cyclops in front of a packed theatre. Known by that time as Sandow, Müller became a sensation.

Unlike other strongmen, who were physically large but often also carried a great deal of bodyfat, Sandow was lean and muscular. He possessed a body almost unknown for his time and was, in effect, one of the earliest modern bodybuilders. Sandow's body was different from other strongmen, he held a strong eye for publicity and his popularity became immense.

From 1889 to 1893, Sandow toured Britain, performing feats of strength, and lecturing on health. Then, in 1893, he travelled to the United States where he spent the next several years. There, his ability to market himself, and his body, grew.

During his time in America, Sandow featured in an early Thomas Edison movie, wrestled a lion, published a book on training and held private posing sessions for the public. Managed by theatre impresario Flo Ziegfeld, Sandow's sold-out shows featured Sandow posing atop a simple cabinet, covered in white chalk, on which he flexed his muscles before lifting heavy objects.[30]

In 1893 Sandow was measured by then director of the Hemenway Gymnasium at Harvard University, Dudley Allen Sargent (1849-1924). Sargent was one of the most important early in helping to turn physical education into a legitimate subject of study in the United States. His system of training, which incorporated both European gymnastics and his exercises was replicated by other well-known physical trainers in the United States like Edward Hartwell, William Anderson, R. Tait McKenize and Luther Gulick. Over the course of his fifty-year career, it is estimated Sargent trained toughly three thousand students from one thousand institutions.[31] He was also a strong advocate for women's physical education and sport.

Of importance here is that Sargent was interested in measuring the determinants of health. He thus measured thousands of men and women be they sporting celebrities, students or the general public. Sargent measured Sandow's body at this time and found that 'there is not the slightest evidence of sham about him.' Sandow's claim to being the world's most perfectly developed specimen was given backing by one of the most prominent voices in fitness!

When Sandow returned to England in 1896 he was ready to expand his interests. In 1898 he founded one of the first fitness magazines in *Physical Culture*. Soon after he published another book on strength (the second of many).

From 1901 until the outbreak of the Great War in 1914, Sandow hosted the world's first modern bodybuilding show, marketed several nutritional supplements, sold children's toys, women's clothing and even opened a 'Curative Institute' of physical culture. Such was Sandow's importance that in 1912 he was appointed Professor of Scientific and Physical Culture to King George V.

Sandow's influence was not confined to Britain or even the United States. During his career, Sandow travelled to Asia, South Africa, Australia, and New Zealand. His books and magazines spread even further afield. Building on the global patterns previously discussed, Sandow's own brand of physical culture was used in countless countries.[32]

Two men inspired by Sandow in the United States, Bernarr Macfadden and Alan Calvert, likewise advanced physical culture's trajectory. Macfadden ran America's largest fitness empire, in the form of *Physical Culture* magazine. Calvert was one of the first largescale manufacturers of barbells and dumbbells.

Calvert founded the Milo Barbell Company in 1902, which as Kim Beckwith found in a study of Calvert, helped revolutionize progressive weight training in the United States. Calvert sold dumbbells, barbells, and kettlebells and also knowledge.[33] In 1914, Calvert created *Strength* magazine, America's first major weight training magazine.[34]

Macfadden and Sandow provide some interesting comparisons, especially because of the physique shows they held in the early 1900s. In 1901 Sandow hosted a 'Great Competition' in London which sought to discover the 'Best Developed Man in Great Britain and Ireland.'

This 'Great Competition' was, in effect, the first modern bodybuilding shows but, unlike modern shows, it had a more holistic selection criterion. Whereas modern bodybuilding focuses on muscle size and symmetry, Sandow's contest focused on skin tone, vitality, and muscular definition.

Macfadden, who hosted shows in 1903/1904 and 1905 at Madison Square Garden in New York, sought to award those with an overall health rather than just the athlete with the biggest muscles. Significantly, Sandow's show was only open to men, whereas Macfadden's shows were open to men and women.[35]

Macfadden also offered the same amount of prize money to men and women. Even today weightlifting, bodybuilding and powerlifting contests tend to offer more money to male competitors, which suggests that Macfadden was ahead of his time.

Unfortunately for him, not everyone shared this enthusiasm. In 1905 Macfadden's second physical culture contest was nearly cancelled after Anthony Comstock, a New York anti-vice activist, argued that the women's contest was pornographic.

On the topic of women's physical culture, Macfadden was perhaps the leading proponent of women's exercise. He held physique contests, wrote on women's exercise, and criticized those who cautioned women against physical activity. His reasons were doing so were rooted in the idea that healthy women would give birth to healthy children.

Several notable strongwomen existed during this period – most notably Katie Brumbach/'Sandwina' (1884–1952), Josephine Schauer Blatt/'Minerva' (1869–1923), and Miriam Kate Williams/'Vulcana' (1874–1946).[36] Women's physical culture was about much more than strongwomen, however, equally important was the expanding role of women in sport and physical education.

In Great Britain, the Ling gymnastics instructor Martina Bergman-Österberg ushered in a revolution in physical training when she founded the Hampstead Physical Training College and Gymnasium in 1885. Hampstead was one of England's first colleges for physical trainers and, significantly, was open only to women.

Sheila Fletcher and Kathleen McCrone's pioneering work on female physical training in England highlighted Hampstead's importance.[37] Not only did it provide qualifications for women in physical training, but several of its graduates also founded their only training colleges. This ensured that women had a place in physical training in England from then on. This practice was mirrored in many parts of Europe and, indeed, Bergman-Österberg was one of many Swedish and Ling trained instructors who travelled Europe during this period.

Also significant in England was the growth of women's sport in the late nineteenth and early twentieth century. While resistance existed, it is significant to note that women's football, cricket, tennis, and cycling – among other sports – began to thrive. Such was the popularity of women's football in England in the early to mid-twentieth century that the English Football Association actually banned women's football in 1921 for fear that its popularity would surpass the men's game.[38]

In the United States, women's physical training and sport likewise experienced a growth, often in previously minor sports. While records of female boxers date to the 1700s, it briefly became a more regular occurrence in the US to the extent that a women's boxing exhibition event was held at the 1904 St. Louis Olympics.[39] Looking at more mainstream practices, women's cycling was deemed a 'craze' in the late nineteenth century but it was only one of many sports. As more women entered universities, they were exposed to sports such as basketball, tennis, swimming, and athletics.

Like the British context, women's physical education also opened up during this time. Returning to Martha Verbrugge, she traced an evolution from 'female frailty' to 'able bodied womanhood' in American physical education during this time.[40] What this meant in practical terms is that more women were exposed to more vigorous forms of exercise – often instructed by a growing cadre of qualified female instructors.

Concurrent with this rise were the opportunities opened up by physical culture. Professor Louis Attila – often deemed the mentor of Eugen Sandow – welcomed female members into his New York gym (which ran from 1898 to 1924). Bernarr Macfadden's Physical Culture magazine was an ardent supporter of women's physical culture and, indeed, was well read by American women.[41]

> ### Problems with the Perfect Body
>
> Sandow and Macfadden's physique shows have often been praised as the beginnings of bodybuilding. While this is arguably true, their shows were problematic from a modern view. Defining what they believed to be the 'ideal body,' both men promoted the lean, athletic, and white physique above all others.
>
> The often-understated racial element of these contests (i.e., that the perfect body was presumed to be white), was replicated in countless later bodybuilding contests. As late as the 1970s athletes of color argued that judges discriminated against them based on their race.
>
> For us, it is a strong reminder that how, and why, we define a 'perfect body' often reveals much about the gender and racial bias of our time.

Sandow and Macfadden's shows strengthened the idea that one could perfect the body, but what about one's strength? The late 1890s and early 1900s were also a vibrant period of weightlifting.

The first major international weightlifting competition was hosted in London in 1891, although several regional shows were held before that point. Weightlifting was even part of the first Olympic Games in Greece in 1896. Over the next decade and a half, the sport went through a significant readjustment period.[42]

Although weightlifting featured at the 1904 games in St. Louis, it was excluded from the 1900, 1908 and 1912 Olympic Games. This 'stop/start' trajectory was based partly on the fact that weightlifting contests were not yet standardized. Nowadays, weightlifting revolves around two lifts, the clean and jerk, and the snatch.

In the early 1900s there was little agreement about which exercises should, and should not, be used in competition. This lack of consistency meant that Olympic organizers were often skeptical about the sport's inclusion.

Weightlifting eventually became standardized in the mid-1920s. For us, now, it is simply important to note its existence and to stress that despite its Olympics exclusion, the sport was growing. By the time of the Great War (1914-1918) then, physical culturists could be prototype bodybuilders, weightlifters, or simply recreational gym users.

On a final note, it is worth stressing that physical culture did not just mean resistance training. Yoga historian Mark Singleton has shown that European and Indian physical culturists in the late nineteenth century began to adopt one another's exercises.[43] In fact, Singleton found specific examples of Indian yogic teachers incorporating exercises from the Ling gymnastics or the bodyweight system of Danish physical culturist J.P. Müller.

The reverse of this was found in physical culture magazines like the British publication *Health & Strength,* which routinely published articles on yoga. Later Indian bodybuilders, like Kolar Venkatesh Iyer, known as K. V. Iyer (1897-1980) synthesized both yoga and resistance training in their writings.[44]

Interwar Physical Culture

The 'Great War' or First World War (1914-1918) had a profound impact on physical culture. The four-year conflict, which resulted in over forty million deaths worldwide, caused a great deal of reflection on the part of governments. The War killed millions of young men which meant, from a geo-political point of view, militaries now had fewer active recruits to call on.

This meant that political parties and governments began to take a much greater interest in physical culture in the inter-war period (1918–1939). The 1920s and 1930s thus saw more time, and money, invested by governments into physical culture.

The most obvious examples of this came in fascist Italy and Germany. In 1922 Benito Mussolini (1883–1945CE) and the National Fascist Party came to power in Italy. A decade later Adolf Hitler (1889–1945CE) led the Nationalist Socialist Party to power in Germany. Establishing authoritarian regimes, and later responsible for untold atrocities, both dictators used physical culture in political ways.

Both governments mandated compulsory physical culture classes for children and adults in the hopes of strengthening male bodies for future conflict. Likewise physical culture was used to project the nation's power. Italian and German governments regularly held large physical culture displays. Containing thousands of men and women, such displays were thought to simultaneously improve patriotism while also serving as a warning to other nations.[45] While this was also the case in the communist Soviet Union, European nations seemed far more concerned with fascist forms of physical culture.[46]

In Germany physical culture was used to reinforce ideas about the ideal German body which, under Nazi racial theory, was white, athletic, and strong. Fascist nations, like Italy and Germany, were shrewd in their use of modern technology, specifically film. Mass gymnastic displays were recorded and played around the world to showcase these nations' strength. Sport was also important for the Nazis. Indeed, the 1936 Olympics hosted in Berlin, Germany, were a celebration of Nazi ideals.

Other nations took notice. It is a strange but true observation to state that many individuals, groups, and countries viewed the Nazi system of physical culture as something to be admired. Despite already worrying signs about discrimination and violence in Germany, Nazi promotion of exercise for all sexes and ages was routinely praised in other parts of Europe and North America during the 1930s.

Great Britain attempted to enact its own physical culture regimen. In 1937 a Physical Training and Recreation Act was passed which sought to improve sport funding, encourage better physical education in schools and promote exercise among the middle-aged.

As Britain still held her Empire, this Act was recreated in several of its dominions. Charlotte MacDonald's work has studied the similarities and differences between the Act in Australia, Canada, and New Zealand. Once again global networks proved pivotal.[47]

But what else was happening during the 1930s? One trend was immediately obvious – an intensification of fitness cultures. Take, for example, the Women's League of Health and Beauty (WLHB). Founded in London in 1930 by Mary Bagot Stack (1883–1935), the League grew from 14 members to over 100,000 global members by 1939. Prior to the outbreak of the Second World War (September 1, 1939), the League had branches in Britain, Ireland, Canada, New Zealand, and several other states.[48]

Aside from its global popularity, the League distinguished itself because of its female-first focus. The League's exercises were designed for, and by, women. Gone were the military exercises or light dumbbells and in their place were exercises from yoga, Ling gymnastics and Bagot Stack's creations.

Seeking to promote 'racial fitness' for all women, which in this context meant white women, the League targeted the young girl and the active grandmother. Class prices were kept artificially low to attract as many members as possible and while the League was deeply concerned about healthy motherhood, it was an indication that women's exercise was evolving.

For men, the 1920s and 1930s witnessed an intensification in fitness. Specifically, sports like weightlifting and bodybuilding finally enjoyed regular and consistent contests. The confusion surrounding weightlifting at the Olympics was solved in the 1920s when it was decided that three exercises would be used in competition.

They were the clean and jerk, the military press, and the snatch. The military press was removed from the Olympics in the 1970s but the clean and the snatch have remained Olympic lifts.[49] This consistency in the exercises used, combined with the introduction of standardized equipment, and weight classes, meant that Olympic weightlifting became recognized as a legitimate sport.

Annual bodybuilding shows were also a feature of this period. In Europe, France, Denmark, and Britain were home to physique competitions at various points, some of which were done entirely through physical culture magazines. It was in the United States, however, where the real changes were happening. The 1920s were a relatively barren period for American bodybuilding. In fact, the only contests of note were two competitions won by Charles Atlas. In 1921 Atlas won an 'America's Most Handsome Man' contest and a 'America's Most Perfectly Developed Man' contest the following year.

Atlas used these victories to fund a mail order workout course in which he promised strength and vitality through his unique system of 'dynamic tension.' With his business partner, Charles Roman, Atlas created one of the most iconic advertisements of the twentieth century, although many of his messages about creating 'new men' were influenced by Earl Liederman, a physical culturist who sold mail-order workout courses in the 1920s.[50]

Titled 'The Insult that Made a Man out of Mac,' advertisements showed a young man being bullied on the beach. Embarrassed by bullies, the man undertakes Atlas' exercises, gets stronger, returns to the beach, and defeats his aggressors. Promising to 'make a man' out of customers, Atlas sold millions of courses.[51]

Atlas claimed his system was based on 'dynamic tension,' a method of building muscles by pitting one muscle of the body against another. Part of this inspiration was said to have come from his visit to the Bronx Zoo wherein Atlas saw an elderly lion stretching. Impressed by the lion's strength – which was gained without dumbbells or barbells, Atlas determined to create his own bodyweight system.

Incidentally, Atlas was not the only man inspired by nature in this regard. Joseph Pilates (1883–1967) of the Pilates system was said to have been inspired by the intuitive movement of cats. Pilates developed his own system when imprisoned in a prisoner of war camp in Britain during the First World War (1914–1918).[52]

It was not until the late 1930s that regular bodybuilding shows were held in America. Change came in 1938 when an individual promoter, Johnny Hordines, hosted a small physique show in Schenectady, New York. Surprised by its popularity, Hordines vowed to run it annually.

At this point the American Athletic Union (AAU) became involved. The AAU oversaw American weightlifting and, as bodybuilding was a tangential sport, took over from Hordines to create a 'Mr. America' contest.

Modelled on the Ms. America pageant (which debuted in 1921), the Mr. America contest was a bodybuilding show dedicated to finding the best representation of American masculinity. Because of this, the show judged contestants on their bodies, personalities, and athleticism.

We will see in the next Chapter how the Mr. America's judging criteria was prejudiced against bodybuilders of color. Here, we will content ourselves in the knowledge that the Mr. America show was the most important title in bodybuilding by the mid-1940s.[53]

On a final note, the inter-war period was a time of great entrepreneurial activity in the United States. We have already discussed Charles Atlas and his mail order 'dynamic tension' course. Equally important was Bob Hoffman (1898–1985) whose York Barbell company became the premier seller of barbells and dumbbells during this period.

Hoffman was a propagandist for physical culture. He used the profits from York Barbell to fund the US Olympic weightlifting team. He founded his own magazine, Strength & Health in 1932 which ran until the 1980s.

In later years he marketed barbells to universities, sports teams, and prisons. He believed in barbells for all, including men, women and even children. Illustrative of this were the many articles and columns he devoted to women's weight training in Strength & Health. The ramifications of this support emerged after the Second World War.[54]

Conclusion

Physical culture, as a phenomenon, was born in the nineteenth century. It was during this century that gymnasium cultures around the world began to resemble and support one another.

Here we traced the evolution of physical culture from the gymnastics of Jahn to the barbells of Bob Hoffman. In a relatively short period of time, exercise moved from callisthenic exercises done for health or to fight, into a sport, a pastime, and a calling.

During the nineteenth century, physical culture could be

divided between multiple camps encompassing the work of the Turners, Ling, Beecher, Lewis, Maclaren, the Sokols and several other training paradigms. Devised for different reasons, these many systems influenced the trajectory of gymnasium cultures.

Prior to the Great War (1914–1918), physical culture was largely an individual phenomenon. During the inter-war period, states began to influence, shape, and dictate the nature of physical activity. Part of this process connected back to Jahn's era when exercise was linked to the state. Individual physical culture still existed, but it now contended with political interests and concerns. For us, such trends highlight the importance of physical culture as a lifestyle and an ideology.

Key Themes from the The Birth of Physical Culture

- The early nineteenth century was pivotal in the development of physical culture.

- The global popularity of gymnasium cultures, and the similarity between these cultures, underpinned the physical culture movement.

- The desire to perfect the body, live in tune with nature, build a healthy life and enjoy greater energy came to dominate physical culture in the late nineteenth and twentieth century.

- During the inter-war period (1918–1939), governments around the world became interested in physical culture. This has continued to the present day.

CHAPTER 4

The Age of Fitness

> *Your goal should be to take your body and make it as healthy, strong, flexible and well-proportioned as you can!*
>
> Jane Fonda Workout Tape, 1981.[1]

As the World emerged from the chaos of the Second World War (1939–1945), changes were afoot societally, politically, and economically. Fitness became even more important in the lives of individuals and in the plans of politicians. As a term, 'physical culture,' began to disappear. In its place were terms like 'bodybuilding,' 'powerlifting,' physical education, and weightlifting. Obviously these terms existed prior to this time, but came to be used with much greater regularity. The language of physical culture changed but its practices remained and strengthened.

From 1945 to the present day, fitness cultures have intensified in their reach and importance. It was during this period that formal physique and strength competitions were created, that supplements were sold, and television programs catered to weight loss and muscle gain emerged. This is to say nothing of the rise of muscle-bound movie stars and, in later years, online influencers.

Examining this phenomenon, we will begin by examining the period 1945 to the early 1960s. Bodybuilding, as a regular sport, began to flourish. It was a time when Olympic weightlifting became a political battleground between the United States and the Soviet Union. Perhaps most importantly, this was a period when anabolic steroids were first used by athletes.

Next the Chapter explores the period from the 1960s to 1980s. This was a period when bodybuilders, like Arnold Schwarzenegger, appeared in Hollywood films and movie stars, like Jane Fonda, made workout tapes. It also witnessed a series of health scares lead to the development of new exercise trends. Also notable were periods of self-reflection surrounding racism and sexism in sports like bodybuilding.

The Chapter ends by discussing changes from the 1990s to the present day. Attention will be drawn here to the formalization of new sports, like women's Olympic weightlifting and CrossFit. This section will focus on the popularity of supplements, changing body expectations for men and women and the growth of gyms in unfamiliar places. The most important development from this era, the rise of social media and the fitness 'influencer' will also be discussed.

New Turns in Post-War Fitness

In the last Chapter we discussed the creation of the Mr. America contest in 1939. Both during and after the Second World War, the Mr. America show was the premier physique contest in the United States. In Europe, similar contests existed like the Mr. Britain award. What distinguished the Mr. America contest from its European counterparts was that its judging system evaluated contestants on their physiques, athleticism, and personality. Despite these differences, bodybuilding was becoming an internationally recognized sport. In 1947 a Mr. Universe title was created and open to competitors from around the globe.[2]

Bodybuilding was growing as a sport, but also as a lifestyle as evidenced by the allure of 'Muscle Beach.' Nowadays Muscle

Beach refers to that strip of land in Venice, California, famed for its gymnasium, skateboarding and alternative cultures. This, however, is the second iteration of Muscle Beach.

Muscle Beach was originally situated in Santa Monica but was closed by the City of Santa Monica in 1958 due to local discontent with its users and a sexual assault case involving two well-known Muscle Beach weightlifters and two underage girls. The case gave the City the opportunity to close the site.[3]

While some Muscle Beach users simply migrated to nearby gyms, others brought its fitness ethos to Venice Beach, where it remains today. From the 1940s to really the present day (with the exception of its closer and informal relocation), Muscle Beach was synonymous with an outdoor lifestyle featuring muscular men and women who lifted weights, performed acrobatics and gymnastics, and worked on their tan. One such woman was Abbye 'Pudgy' Stockton (1917–2006) who is largely regarded as a forerunner of modern female bodybuilders and weightlifters.

Alongside her husband Les, Pudgy was famous for hand balancing and weightlifting feats at Muscle Beach. She became a common feature in weightlifting magazines and, in time, was given her own training column in Bob Hoffman's *Strength and Health* magazine.

Entitled 'Barbelles,' the column was foundational for women's strength and bodybuilding cultures. Begun in 1944, the column ran for a decade. Within it, Pudgy published images of female weightlifters and bodybuilders, gave nutritional advice and, helped, in part, to normalize the practice of women lifting weights.

Such was Pudgy's influence that in 1947 she organized a women's weightlifting contest. While sanctioned women's weightlifting contests did not truly come until the 1970s, Pudgy's early efforts were significant. In 1948, Pudgy was awarded a 'Miss Physical Culture Venus' award by Bernarr Macfadden in honor of her strength and physique.[4] These two worlds, weightlifting, and bodybuilding, were briefly embodied by Pudgy.

Pudgy was not the only woman of the 1930s and 1940s to lift weights. In England Ivy Russell helped organize strength contests and even initiated the creation of a women's weightlifting association. It was Pudgy, however, who exerted the most influence through her magazine columns and regular appearances in recorded media.

What undoubtedly helped Pudgy in this regard was the idealized picture of Muscle Beach in American culture during these decades. While the reality was not often as glamorous as it seemed, the idea of 'Muscle Beach' facilitated a new muscle building lifestyle that savvy entrepreneurs exploited.

It is at this point we turn to the Weider Brothers, Joe (1919–2013) and Ben (1923–2008). Born in Montreal, Canada, the Weiders came to dominate the sport of bodybuilding during the mid-twentieth century. They sold magazines, supplements, books, sponsored bodybuilders and created bodybuilding's most important contest in 1965, the Mr. Olympia.

Founding a series of bodybuilding magazines in Canada in the 1940s, the Weiders moved their business interests to the United States soon after. There the Weiders competed against Bob Hoffman of York Barbell for the next several decades.

Bob Hoffman was an advocate for Olympic weightlifting and promoted that sport above all else. While he did branch into bodybuilding, notably the Mr. America show, he was known as a weightlifter. The Weiders, on the other hand were outright proponents of bodybuilding.

Where Hoffman had his followers – in their hundreds of thousands – the Weiders targeted a growing number of men who were unconcerned with weightlifting and more interested in building the body above all else. They wrote on new muscle building techniques, created bodybuilding shows and deliberately stole Hoffman's customers.[5]

Despite their later success, the Weiders, and other smaller entrepreneurs, could not displace Hoffman during the 1940s and 1950s for one simple reason – he was too powerful. York Barbell was the most successful workout manufacturer of the age and Hoffman was celebrated within the weightlifting community.

From 1936 to 1960, Hoffman was the coach of the American Olympic weightlifting team during their most successful period.[6] He trained athletes, gave many of them jobs within York Barbell and was a propagandist for the sport's importance. Hoffman believed that America's weightlifting success was emblematic of the nation's cultural and economic power.[7]

Hoffman's athletes secured over 30 Olympic weightlifting medals and many more at World Championships. The team won an Olympic medal at every weightlifting class during the 1956 Games (4 golds, 2 silvers, 1 bronze). What distinguished the American team from its competitors?

The Melting Pot Myth?

Aside from the economic advantages present in the United States when compared to its European or Asian rivals in the post-Second World War period, Hoffman claimed that his team's greatest strength came from its cultural integration. Hoffman's Olympic weightlifters were often second-generation immigrants in the United States with family ties to Japan, Italy, Poland, and many other regions.

> Hoffman claimed that America was the only team which could compete with African American weightlifters competing alongside Japanese Americans, competing alongside Italian Americans. This was part of the 'American dream' and the reasons for America's success.
>
> Work on Bob Hoffman's Strength and Health magazine explained that although Hoffman was a firm supporter of his athletes, his magazines nevertheless treated his African American athletes (like weightlifter John Davies) different from Caucasian weightlifters.[8] This included racialized depictions and insensitive language. As is perhaps a recurring theme in this handbook, the reality is often very different from the ideal.
>
> Hoffman claimed a post-racial team, but his magazines provided anything but.

Hoffman offered many reasons for his team's success, but he rarely mentioned the importance of timing. In the 1940s, other nations didn't have the resources, or ability, of competing with the United States. When other teams caught up, however, his team's fortunes changed. This was especially the case with the Soviet Union.

In 1952, the Soviet Union (USSR) entered its first Olympic Games since the Russian Empire competed in the 1912 Games. Initially the USSR (which emerged from the 1917 Russian Revolution and expanded post-1945) refused to compete in the Olympics as they believed sporting competition upheld the capitalist system which the Communist USSR opposed.

Eventually, a decision was taken to enter the Olympics with the intention of winning as many medals as possible. Just like Hoffman, the USSR sought to use the Olympics to display its own power, and the success of the Communist system. State-sponsored sporting programs were created in the USSR with the express intention of earning Olympic gold.

The USSR provided greater support for athletes than the United States. Soviet weightlifters were better fed, had more time to train and were given greater support. This was the perfect formula for success. Within three Olympic cycles (1952 to 1960), the USSR won more medals than America. America's dominance evaporated.

The Soviets had better coaching networks but also had a chemical advantage. In 1954, the medical doctor for the weightlifting team, Dr. John Ziegler, met with his Russian counterpart at the World Weightlifting Championships. There, Ziegler was told about that Soviet weightlifters were using synthetic testosterone to improve their strength.

Intrigued, Ziegler returned to America and began work on an American equivalent. In 1958 he created an anabolic steroid, 'Dianabol' or 'DBOL' with the pharmaceutical firm Ciba. DBOL became the first major steroid in fitness circles among weightlifters, then bodybuilders and then the public.[9]

Importantly, anabolic steroids were introduced at the same moment that nutritional supplements were first marketed in fitness magazines. The next section will discuss the ramifications that this co-emergence had in fitness cultures for men and women.

From Pumping Iron to Getting Physical

By end of the 1950s fitness cultures were home to anabolic steroids, nutritional supplements, ever expanding fitness programs, and regular bodybuilding contests. Where the previous decades were dominated by Olympic weightlifting, especially at a political level, the next two decades belonged to the bodybuilders.

The reasons for this were simple – bodybuilders grew in numbers, and in size. The anabolic steroids introduced into Olympic weightlifting during the 1950s quickly found their way into bodybuilding circles. Indeed, it is remarkable to compare the physiques of bodybuilders in the 1930s or 1940s to those in the 1970s.

The size and leanness of later bodybuilders was indicative of their steroid usage. The general fitness public was often ignorant to this fact. At that time scientists and doctors were still unsure of the muscle-building properties of steroids.

So too were athletes. Randy Roach found at least one instance in which a famous bodybuilder claimed steroids made them lose muscle![10] What really fueled this ignorance, however, was the creation of nutritional supplements by people like Bob Hoffman and Joe Weider.

In 1950 nutritionist Irvin Johnson (later called Rheo H. Blair) published an article in *Ironman* magazine entitled 'Build Bigger Biceps Faster with Food Supplements.' Soon after Johnson, began selling soy protein powders in Hoffman's *Strength and Health* magazine.

Within a decade Hoffman, Weider, Blair, and countless other entrepreneurs sold nutritional supplements which promised to build muscle fast, strip away unwanted fat and provide unbounding health. While such claims were often refuted by the American government's regulation body, the Food and Drug Administration

(FDA), the FDA lacked the power to target unfounded nutritional claims.[11]

Fitness supplements were sold to the public, using steroid using bodybuilders as models, and making steroid like claims about products. Little has changed in the fitness industry!

> ### What Supplements Do You Take and Why?
>
> Globally nutritional and health supplements are a billion-dollar industry, popular among every group across the life cycle. Many people, this author included, have taken a supplement (be it protein powders, fish oils, creatine, vitamins/minerals, etc.) in the hope of attaining a promised benefit.
>
> Do you take supplements? And, if so, why? Do they provide the benefits they promise?

'Supplements and steroids' is a useful way of describing bodybuilding from the 1960s to the present day, but this labelling does not capture the full story. Equally important were the proliferation of bodybuilding contests. What become the most important of these shows was the Mr. Olympia contest, created by, Joe and Ben Weider in 1965.

Previously the Mr. America contest was the sport's premier trophy. By the early 1960s, however, many bodybuilders had grown tired and resentful of its judging process. In focusing on athleticism, personality and then the body, the contest was thought to be subject to the whims of individual judges.

This was problematic for Black, African American, and Hispanic competitors, many of whom won the physique component but lost on their personalities. Accusations of racism were levelled against the contest for several years and reached a crescendo in the early 1960s when Cuban bodybuilder Sergio Oliva claimed that AAU (the body who oversaw the contest) didn't know the American Civil War was over.

Suspicions that Caucasian bodybuilders were favored were combined with restrictive entrance rules (winners of the Mr. America were not allowed to re-enter). Although Chris Dickerson became the first Black and gay Mr. America champion in 1970, many bodybuilders were dissatisfied with the kinds of contests on offer.[12]

The Mr. Olympia, which is still regarded as the ultimate prize in men's bodybuilding, differentiated itself from the Mr. America in two ways. Anyone could enter (including previous winners) and it judged contestants on their physiques.

The move to outright bodybuilding marked a significant change in the fitness community of the 1960s but it was not the only one. Societally, in the United States and elsewhere, previously uninterested individuals took to health practices to maintain, and improve, their physical health.

The 1960s and 1970s was a period when many Western societies became increasingly worried about heart disease. Just like modern concerns many societies exhibit around obesity, politicians, and public health officers tried to tackle the scourge of heart disease plaguing men and women.

In the United States heart disease was the most common form of death in the 1960s. The first real sign that heart disease was a public health concern came in 1955 when then U.S. President Dwight Eisenhower had a near fatal heart attack while in office.

Eisenhower was known as a strong, vibrant, and powerful personality. The shock surrounding his condition signaled that no one was immune from heart disease. Plans were devised to increase exercise among the public and reform the American diet.

Eisenhower went on to form the first version of the President's Council on Physical Fitness in 1956. At the time Eisenhower was motivated in part by his own heart attack but, more substantially, by Cold War era concerns.[13]

A defining feature of the Cold War was the constant comparison between the United States and the Soviet Union be it economically, politically or in the sporting world. During this period, there were fears that America was falling behind the Soviet Union in terms of its health. Such concerns were supported by an influential study by Dr. Hans Kraus and Bonnie Prudden.

Kraus was an Associate Professor of Physical Medicine and Rehabilitation at the time of the study. Prudden was the Director of the Institute for Physical Fitness at White Plains. Dealing with the President in 1955, the duo reported that – based upon their own findings – American children were weaker than their European counterparts, were not as physically fit and were inflexible.[14]

Famously described by *Sport Illustrated* as 'The Report that Shocked the President,' the Kraus and Prudden study, and the 'Kraus-Weber' test used to study children's fitness, were the primary motivation behind the President's Council. The Council's influence over American physical culture has waxed and waned in subsequent decades but it did help to shape school physical education curricula and increase the attention given to children's fitness.[15]

The desire to alleviate and prevent heart disease was not just the concern of government officials. Individual coaches and trainers also began creating their own programs. One such solution was the act of 'jogging.' Yes, 'jogging' is a relatively new creation which stemmed from mid-twentieth-century concerns about the heart.

Running was not new. After all, running was contested at the

1896 Athens Olympics and the Boston marathon was first held in 1897. Prior to that track events were found at the Caledonian games, athletics competitions were plentiful, and, in some instances, celebrity runners existed. This is to say nothing of the popularity that pedestrianism (competitive walking) had during the eighteenth and nineteenth century.[16] Yet prolonged running, at a moderate pace, was not something that the public typically did.

In 1961, New Zealand marathon runner Arthur Lydiard created an Auckland running club with a simple interest in mind – running at an easy pace to improve heart health. What began with a small group of people exploded into a running sensation. Lydiard gained an international reputation which attracted supporters from around the world.

One such individual was Bill Bowerman – co-founder of Nike. Bowerman visited Lydiard in the early 1960s and when he returned to the United States, published a small four-page pamphlet on jogging. Sponsored by the Oregon Heart Foundation and The US National Bank of Portland, *The Joggers Manual,* as it was titled, aimed to spread the message of jogging.

What truly launched the jogging phenomenon was Kenneth Cooper and his 1968 book *Aerobics* (which incidentally launched the mainstream use of this word). A former physician for the Air Force, Cooper's prescription that individuals run for fifteen to twenty minutes to protect themselves against heart disease, improve their health and boost their productivity helped spark the jogging movement initiated by those before him.[17]

Owing to his medical background, Cooper's means of measuring fitness and health prescriptions provided a certainty about jogging's benefits. Some of you may even have experienced the 'Cooper Test' (a twelve-minute running test Cooper devised to test aerobic fitness) during your schooling.

Jogging became an international sensation, practiced by

people across the life cycle. In the United States, its demographic eventually moved from middle-aged men and women interested in preserving their health to younger generations interested in looking good and alternative lifestyles. Showing its malleability, jogging was popularized with the 'hippie movement' of the 1970s.[18]

Equally transformative was the prevalence of the feminist movement in the United States. In a sporting context, the feminist movement achieved its greatest success through the passing of the Title IX Act in 1972 which prohibited sex-based discrimination in educational programs which received federal money.

Simplified this meant that women's sport, in educational settings, gained a greater amount of funding than ever before. This resulted in greater participation rates and a sense among some that women could compete in many more sports.[19]

The late 1970s and early 1980s witnessed the creation of female competitions in sports like bodybuilding, powerlifting and, in time, Olympic weightlifting. An early organizer, and competitor, of women's bodybuilding, Doris Barrilleaux, later told Professor Jan Todd and Désirée Harguess, of the inspiration she found in the feminist movement.[20]

Likewise, Jan Todd, who later became a professor of physical culture, was an influential figure in the creation of women's powerlifting. Todd, alongside individuals like Dr. Cindy Wyatt Reinhoudt, helped write the rules for women's powerlifting while simultaneously competing in it. For those unfamiliar with it, powerlifting is a test of strength wherein competitors attempt to lift the heaviest weight across three lifts – the bench press, the deadlift, and the squat.

The first male sanctioned powerlifting meet was in 1964. A female powerlifting contest was held in 1977 while it took until 1987 for a World Weightlifting Contest to feature female athletes. The need to push for equality (which still exists) can be seen as a byproduct of third-wave feminism and the consequence of physical culture's growing popularity.[21]

Something that was helping to drive this popularity was the influence of television and film. In 1951 Jack Lalanne was given his own fitness program on television, which ran for the next several decades. Lalanne's was not the first fitness show, but it was the most popular. In the 1950s and 1960s bodybuilders and physique stars began appearing in mainstream television shows and films.

Take, for example, Reg Park and Steve Reeves, two bodybuilders who both starred in Hercules films at this time. When talking about star bodybuilders, it would be remiss not to mention Arnold Schwarzenegger (b. 1947), the Austrian born bodybuilder who won seven Mr. Olympias, starred in multiple movies, became Governor of California and organized the Arnold Festival in Columbus, Ohio.[22]

Arnold's breakout role came in *Pumping Iron* (1977), a bodybuilding documentary which achieved mainstream success. As a film *Pumping Iron* helped drive thousands of men and women into gyms. Many of the studies on bodybuilding in the 1980s cited *Pumping Iron* as responsible for a new growth in gym numbers.[23]

Pumping Iron was also significant in helping to popularize Gold's Gym, the primary gym used in the film. Opened by Joe Gold in 1965, and sold to Bud Danits in 1970, Gold's Gym went through several owners by the time of *Pumping Iron*. Its inclusion in the documentary helped to build the gym's own brand. Indeed, it became a popular tourist trap for aspiring muscle builders. While Gold's Gym eventually branched out into a domestic, and then an international franchise, it wasn't the first gym brand in the United States.[24]

From the 1940s to the late 1950s, Vic Tanny, and his chain of gyms were the most recognizable American fitness hubs. Tanny's business model at the time was simple. He sold affordable gym memberships with very aggressive sales tactics. Tanny held the first major national gym chain but, owing to poor management, and misleading advertisements, they began to close in the early 1960s.

Tanny's legacy lived on in obvious, and more subtle ways. A former Tanny employee, Rudy Smith, later went on to open the Holiday Spa chain, which some consider to be the most successful health chain ever.[25] A former trainee in a Vic Tanny club, Arthur Jones, later revolutionized the practice of training with machines when he opened *Nautilus* gyms in the 1970s.

Nautilus was the name Arthur gave to the exercise machines he designed, first sold in 1970. Jones was a master of promotion and, in advertising his machines, claimed to have designed the most effective method of exercising – one far more beneficial than free weight training or aerobics. Using a very distinct form of design, which kept constant pressure on the muscle, Jones' machines were more accessible for the public because they were easy to use.

In time, Jones, and his affiliates, opened *Nautilus* only gyms, in which trainees exercised in a circuit – moving from one machine to the next. Jones' machines were not the only training advances in this regard, Harold Zinkin's Universal machines were likewise popular, but his entrepreneurism set him apart.[26]

Jones, alongside Joe Weider and Bob Hoffman, helped convince athletes to weight train during this period. Likewise, Jones was an early supporter of the National Strength and Conditioning Association (founded in 1978), which was the first American body for strength and conditioning coaches.[27]

On new training styles, it is important to note that it wasn't all about Jones. In 1982 actor Jane Fonda starred in a home workout tape *'Jane Fonda's Workout.'* Sold as a VHS tape, the workout ignited both the home fitness and aerobics craze of the 1980s.[28] Away from barbells and dumbbells, countless gym goers went to new fitness studios to perform step aerobics, calisthenic classes and use light dumbbells. This pattern continues today if one considers that Zumba classes date to the mid-1990s.

Likewise, from the 1960s onward, meditation and yoga in the West became increasingly incorporated into people's physical culture regimens. During this period, well known Asian teachers, like B.K.S. Iyengar and others became popular in the West. Yoga's popularity strengthened in the 1980s when physicians like Dean Ornish (a well-known advocate of plant based diets) and others connected yoga to proven health benefits.[29] Returning to Mark Singleton, he cited the 1990s as a period when yoga became the commercial enterprise in the West that it continues to be.[30]

All in all, the period from the 1950s to the late 1980s was the moment when physical culture and fitness projects went from a small but significant sub-culture to part of the mainstream itself.

Modern Physical Culture

At the time of writing, it is estimated that the gym industry is worth over $96 billion U.S. dollars worldwide.[31] Similarly, the nutritional supplement market is valued at roughly $167.8 billion.[32] Speaking in general terms, fitness cultures have become remarkably accessible and popular since the 1990s. Anecdotally, during the writing of this book, I exercised in hotels, franchise gyms, airports, universities, home gyms, outdoor exercise classes, my back garden, and sports clubs.

Such locations illustrate the variety of ways in which fitness has become a necessity of modern life for many, rather than a hobby. With that in mind, this section is going to discuss some of the ways in which fitness cultures have grown since the 1990s.

What better place to begin than the supplement industry? Prior to 1990 nutritional supplements tended to revolve around protein powders, weight gainers, vitamins, and minerals. At times, new efforts like Dan Duchaine's *Ultimate Orange* pre-workout (first produced in 1982) were sold, but the supplement industry was relatively static.

That changed during the 1990s and early 2000s when new products, some of which were subsequently banned, were introduced. This was not without controversy. In the early 1990s creatine was first sold to gym-goers as a supplement that would improve endurance and strength.

Despite evidence to the contrary, creatine was depicted by many news outlets during the 1990s as an illegal substance. In fact, several researchers have noted a 'creatine scare' at this time – especially after several high-profile articles were published in the United States.[33] The media's concern, which extended to parents, teachers, and physicians, was in some ways understandable.

The 1990s was also a time when performance enhancing drugs became notably more prevalent. What was once the preserve of athletes was now being used by the average gym goer. The previously mentioned pre-workout manufacturer, Dan Duchaine, was a key figure in this process.

In 1981, Duchaine produced *The Underground Steroid Handbook*. Such was its popularity that it underwent several revisions in later years. Duchaine was, for many, the face of recreational and professional steroid use. Although his heyday was the 1990s, he was not the only individual to revolutionize steroid use.[34]

In 2001, chemist Patrick Arnold marketed prohormones among the fitness community. Initially sold as a legal supplement, prohormones spiked testosterone levels and hence produced steroid like effects. Many of these substances were banned in the United States following the passage of the Anabolic Steroid Control Act of 2004 and were subsequently banned worldwide.[35]

Nevertheless, the tendency for supplement manufacturers to include illegal substances in products has continued to grow. This is especially the case with pre-workout supplements, which enjoyed renewed popularity from the 2010s onwards. Repeated stories of illicit substances, including meth amphetamines, being included in products highlights a need for skepticism around supplements.[36]

The growth of supplements which border on illegal reflected the changed landscape of muscle building. From the 1980s onwards professional bodybuilders began to experiment with new and harsher performance enhancing drugs. Diuretics, human growth hormone and insulin were regularly used to push the boundaries of the human body.

This had broader ramifications. In 2000 Harvard psychiatrist Harrison Pope, Katharine Phillips and Roberto Olivardia published *The Adonis Complex* which found that young men felt increasingly pressurized to display six pack abdominals, large arms, etc. This pressure to conform to fit and muscular ideals was pushing members of the public into using anabolic steroids.[37]

It would, of course, be trite to mention male body ideals without noting fitness messages for women. Where men were becoming pressurized to become muscular, women in the fitness space faced several contradictory views.

Bodybuilder and scholar Leslie Heywood previously explained that women have long been taught that slim and delicate physiques were the most desirable. This message influenced female physical culture where, even in the 1990s, women were encouraged to build some muscle but not too much.[38] But what, you are no doubt wondering about women's bodybuilding?

Women's bodybuilding during the 1990s – and to the present day – was plagued with criticisms that overly muscular women were masculine and hence the sport was 'grotesque.' Such messages came from magazines but also from organizers. In 2005, the organizers of the Ms. Olympia contest (first held in 1980) asked contestants to reduce their size and muscularity by 20% to avoid criticisms of being too masculine.

Heywood, and many Ms. Olympia winners, have cited a double standard on the part of organizers whose ideas are rooted in outdated and contradictory ideas about what a woman's body should look like.[39]

Unfortunately for professional female bodybuilders, the Ms. Olympia organizers continued to attack 'excessive' female muscularity. Other divisions were introduced and, in 2014 the contest was discontinued. The sport was saved thanks to a new organization called Wings of Strength (WOS) which provided a platform for athletes. Eventually the Ms. Olympia was revived in 2020.

Women's Olympic weightlifting which, despite becoming a sanctioned event in the 1970s, had to wait until 2000 to appear at an Olympic Games. Remember from previous chapters that men's Olympic weightlifting was first held in 1896. Since 2000 women's Olympic weightlifting has continued to progress as athletes receive the support they need.

A World Strongest Woman contest was held in 1997 (two decades after the first World Strongest Man contest in 1977). What distinguishes strongman and strongwoman contests from other sports is that the World Strongest Man contest is a television show produced by Trans World International while World Strongest Woman is a privately funded and organized contest.

One fitness trend from this period which did offer equality to male and female participants was CrossFit. In 2000 Greg

Glassman and Lauren Jenai founded CrossFit, a system which promised to build holistic health by training athletes through a variety of paradigms.

Incorporating exercises from bodybuilding, weightlifting, powerlifting, and calisthenics, CrossFit promised to build exercisers who were strong but aerobically fit. In essence, CrossFit was created in reaction to dominant fitness trends.

In 2007 a CrossFit Games was created to act as a competition to determine the fittest and strongest male and female athlete. The prize monies offered to men and women were the same, which was a rare mark of equality in a typically unbalanced fitness field.[40] At the time of writing, CrossFit has also become a hub of important conversations about sex and race.

In 2020 CrossFit CEO Greg Glassman resigned following an online Twitter post in which Glassman appeared to mock the Covid-19 pandemic and the George Floyd tragedy within the United States. As a Black man, Floyd's death at the hand of a Minnesota police officer in 2020 forced multiple conversations about race in America.

Glassman's tweet resulted in CrossFit losing sponsorships and, more importantly, a vocal outcry on the part of BIPOC CrossFitters who refused to associate with the company.[41] Since then the CrossFit community has made a clear effort to elevate previously marginalized groups.

While it is impossible to know whether such changes will be permanent it is telling that CrossFit is now attempting to create inclusive spaces regardless of race or sexuality. Yet again, this marks CrossFit as different from more traditional fitness spaces which, as we have repeatedly discussed, have tended to be conservative. Conservativism aside, the last twenty years, in particular, have seen a much greater number of women take to weight training and bodybuilding, yoga, spin classes, aerobics and general fitness classes. CrossFit was and is an obvious example.

To end, it is worth noting the importance of the internet and social media in fitness. From the early 2000s internet forums and blogs have become the primary means through which exercisers gather information. While this has led to an increase in knowledge and has wrestled the control of information away from manufacturers and magazine publishers, it has also led to a great deal of miscommunication and harm.[42]

More positively, the internet has facilitated greater communication between exercise scientists and the public. Whereas previously academic studies tended to remain unknown to the public, a significant number of academics have created websites, podcasts, e-books, and forums to allow for the discussion of evidence-based practices. Misinformation still reigns, but the ability to objectively evaluate the efficacy of supplements, training programs and nutritional plans has helped strip some of the mystique away from peddlers of dangerous or defunct knowledge.

Conclusion

After the Second World War (f. 1945), physical culture became splintered and fragmented. This was undoubtedly for the better. This fragmentation led to the opening out of fitness cultures from the sub-culture to the mainstream. Whereas physical culturists were a small but dedicated number in the early 1900s, it is no exaggeration to say that now many people are at least familiar with the health field.

Not all change has been positive, of course. The introduction of anabolic steroids into the fitness sphere in the 1950s and 1960s had grave ramifications for male and female physiques in a variety of sports and contexts.

Steroids inadvertently supported the supplement industry. Nutritional supplements, from protein powders to pre-workout supplements are renowned for promising 'steroid-like' effects, and for using enhanced athletes in advertising.

The 1940s to the present-day have been chaotic for the fitness industry and defy an easy summary. The best we can possibly do is to note a general opening, or 'democratization,' of fitness. Prejudices still exist but the allure of health and physical culture has never been stronger.

Key Themes from The Age of Fitness

- The 1940s and 1950s was defined by the battle between Bob Hoffman and Joe Weider, and the American versus the Soviet weightlifting teams. These rivalries advanced bodybuilding and weightlifting.

- The period 1940 to 2000 was characterized by an evolution and formalization of fitness cultures. That bodybuilding, powerlifting, strength contests and CrossFit were created during this period highlights physical culture's variety and popularity.

- Anabolic steroids were first used by weightlifters and, from there, became commonplace among the fitness industry.

- 'Third wave feminism' in the 1960s and 1970s helped open doors to women in the fitness industry as evidenced by the creation of women's bodybuilding shows, powerlifting meets and Olympic weightlifting.

- Social media, and the internet, helped to spread information and misinformation among the fitness industry. The effects of this development have yet to be fully realized.

CONCLUSION

The Past, Present and Future of Physical Culture

Are we all physical culturists? In a fascinating chapter, written several years ago, sociologist Niall Richardson asked this same question about bodybuilding. Writing on his teaching practices, Richardson noted that a question he often asks students is what is, and is not, bodybuilding?[1] Using a wide definition – which effectively amounted to all efforts made to enhance the body's appearance – Richardson claimed everything from diet to tattooing could fall under bodybuilding activities.

Could the same be true for physical culture? After all, modern society has increasingly viewed the body as a project, one in need of constant maintenance and care. This explains, in part, the profitability found in both the fitness and nutritional supplement industry. To truthfully answer whether we are all physical culturists however, we do need to define what we mean.

In the introduction we noted how difficult a term physical culture is to define. Hopefully this confusion still exists in your mind. Physical culture defies an easy explanation, as do the reasons underpinning its popularity across millennia. Do we describe it as bodybuilding activities? Or efforts designed to improve one's cardiovascular health? What about training soldiers?

How we define physical culture, and hence answer whether we are physical culturists, depends entirely on the period we are discussing. An easier task is to describe physical culture practices, which, as we have discussed, have always revolved around strengthening bodies, enhancing physiques, increasing endurance, enhancing health, fighting against aging, and becoming better athletes.

Physical culture practices have existed for thousands of years but not always for the same motivations. In this short handbook, we have explored some of the reasons men and women have taken to physical culture practices across millennia. Here I want to briefly run through some of these motivations before ending with some more speculative comments.

In discussing the motivations for physical culture, it is useful to distinguish between the ancient, pre-modern and modern worlds, and to highlight what similarities and differences existed between all three periods.

Speaking in general terms, physical culture practices in the Ancient World were done for three keys reasons – to become better soldiers or athletes, for spiritual reasons, and for medical reasons. Military training is perhaps the primary reason why physical culture thrived in the Ancient World and why it survived into the following centuries.

Training for warfare necessitated strong and fit soldiers, hence the need for strengthening exercises. It is odd to consider the importance of the military in general fitness cultures but, for trainees in the Ancient World, the two went hand in hand. Away from the military we discussed exercise's importance in religious practices, wherein training was used to honor the dead or in prayer.

Physical culture also served a key component in health and medical contexts, where physical activity was prescribed to avoid, or recover from, an illness. In certain areas, and eras, physical culture was used in an educational context and, in some rare instances, as a test of one's physical fitness to rule over others.

The importance of the military and military fitness continued to be important in the Middle Ages, the Renaissance, and the Enlightenment. What differed between these periods was educational, recreational, and medicinal physical culture. In the Middle Ages, societal and religious pressure largely disbarred physical culture practices.

Although knights were celebrated for their strength and training, the individual man or woman was rarely permitted to indulge in these practices. This changed, of course, in the Renaissance and the Enlightenment when schools and physicians once more came alive to the value that physical fitness had in sustaining mind, body and soul.

During the Renaissance and Enlightenment physical training came to be used in schools to bring a more holistic education for children. This was a return to the 'whole mind/whole body' ethos that Europeans believed defined Ancient Greek education.

As children became adults, they took to gymnasiums cultures. We can say that a critical mass was being approached wherein fitness was becoming more and more commonplace. This underpinned the 'birth of physical culture' in the late nineteenth and early twentieth century.

Physical culture marked an era in history (c. 1880s-1940s) when societies around the world began to celebrate and promote physical fitness and gym cultures in a much greater way than ever before. Fitness cultures further intensified in schools, militaries, recreational spaces and everywhere in between. There was also the beginning of fitness celebrities like Eugen Sandow, who is still regarded as the 'Father' of modern bodybuilding.

From physical culture, which intensified in the interwar period (1918-1939), there was the splitting of fitness into various activities in the mid-twentieth century. What was once called physical culture was next labelled as bodybuilding, weightlifting, powerlifting, aerobics, etc.

We still live within this age with the exception that social media and the internet have magnified many of the concerns and motivations found in previous decades. Undoubtedly the internet has provided more information about health and wellbeing, but this transformation has not always been positive.

This is the general trajectory of this book. Hopefully it looks familiar to you by now. Without confusing things too much, I now want to raise two points about the above narrative.

> 1) <u>We must be careful of assuming that everything is progress:</u> If we follow the above narrative too closely, we might assume that our modern climate marks the epitome of human history and fitness. Put another way, we may think that our fitness cultures are the most popular, scientific, and important than at any other point in history. It is best to be humble, especially given that our knowledge of the Ancient World is far from conclusive.
>
> 2) <u>Grand narratives often ignore human experiences:</u> The above history is useful, but it ignores the lived experience of the people themselves. We know people exercised in Ancient Athens, in Middle Age France, in Enlightenment England and in 1960s America. What we don't know is why they exercised, how it felt to them and what place it held in their lives.

So, we know people exercised across centuries and millennia. What did health or the perfect body mean for them? This varied on the time, place, and society of the exercisers. For those studying the body, it is important to highlight the multiplicity of meanings people ascribe to physical culture.

Some of the key themes – both personal and societally – that we discussed related to:

- Warfare
- Religion
- Race
- Medicine
- Gender
- Education
- Commercialism
- Popular Culture
- Sport
- Politics

These mark just some of the reasons how, and why, people and societies took to physical activity. What is important to note here is that although the exercises often differed across societies, the reasons often remained the same.

Whatever new developments come in the history of physical culture, it is important that we return again and again to the motivations and broader social trends underpinning the next way of concerns and fears surrounding the body. Speculating, somewhat, it is likely that the fitness community will continue to divide and specialize based upon individual desires.

A positive phenomenon in the past decade has been the awareness that multiple body shapes and sizes exist. Whether this relates to the body acceptance moment, awareness of ageism, or the rising recognition of disability sport, the fitness space is being forced to confront the previously restrictive models it promoted as ideal.

Likewise, the proliferation of information on the internet and social media means that now, more than ever, information on healthy eating and exercise habits is available in previously heralded waves. The average gym goer now has more available knowledge than a professor of exercise scientist had in the 1950s or 1960s. This is a positive.

The downside of this, of course, is the potential to spread misinformation or dangerous ideas. Restrictive diets, problematic body goals and the sale of illegal bodybuilding drugs online are all issues in the fitness space. Much like the spread of good information, it is likely that bad information will continue to spread in online spaces.

Finally, the biggest point of concern on the part of governments is undoubtedly the issue of obesity, diabetes, high blood pressure, and other non-communicable diseases. While some debates about obesity amount to nothing more than body shaming, a far more real issue has been the lack of physical activity now found across many parts of the world.

The past two decades has seen both the World Health Organization and individual governments attempt to increase physical activity among populations.[2] Much like the 'heart disease scare' of the 1950s and 1960s which we previously discussed, current debates revolve around panicked ideas that the rising generation is unhealthy, and in need of intervention.

Looking into a crystal ball, it is likely the next few decades will see a tension between personal health and the government's role in promoting wellbeing. What this will look like is difficult to know, but there is little doubt that the motivations that have endured across time – those present in both Ancient China and modern America – will exist in the background of debates.

Summing Up ...

Writing this book was one of the most rewarding, and challenging, tasks of my academic career. As someone who writes a great deal on the history of physical culture, and teaches it to lucky/unlucky students, the task of condensing this history into a shortened form was the toughest of all workouts.

Ideally this book would end on a rousing statement about the need to continue studying and contributing to the history of physical culture. That seems rather trite given that the purpose of this handbook, at least its aim, is to invite you to scrutinize messages about the body and physical activity.

We also need to think about what was not included in this book. Owing to reasons of expediency, this handbook focused primarily on British and American physical culture. European physical culture occasionally emerged, but our focus on Asian, African, and South American physical culture was limited after the first Chapter.

This does not mean that such cultures did not have their own vibrant physical cultures. Likewise we did not discuss the emergence of powerlifting in the Special Olympics or Paralympics. Inattention here does not mean it was not important.

Why do people train? How do people train and what can we learn about these trends? In 1933 British physical culturist Alfred Danks wrote,

> No single piece of machinery, however scientifically designed or intricately it may be devised can, even remotely compare with the human body...[3]

The purity of his wonder at the human body cannot be faulted. My body, your body and everyone else's' bodies are truly miracles and should be treated with reverence and wonder for doing something as simple as blinking.

That we often treat the body as an afterthought, as something in the background of our lives means that we are often ignorant about the messages and pressures we place on that body. I hope, truly, that this handbook has demonstrated the rich, and at times unpleasant, history that efforts to physically change the body have had. Never forget that our bodies, and our ideas about what a body should or could do, reflect our very societies, our deepest desires and our philosophical belief in what it means to be human.

NOTES

Introduction

1. The Stark Center, 'About the Center,' https://starkcenter.org/about/. The Stark Center is one of the few institutions dedicated to the study, and conversation, of the history of physical culture. Many of the historians discussed in this book have official or unofficial links to the Center.
2. Jan Todd, *Physical Culture and the Body Beautiful: Purposive Exercise in the Lives of American Women, 1800-1870* (Macon: Mercer University Press, 1998), 3-5.
3. According to Jan Todd the term physical culture was first used in relation to physical activity in the eighteenth-century. Jan Todd, 'Reflections on Physical Culture: Defining Our Field and Protecting Its Integrity,' *Iron Game History* 13, no. 2-3 (2015): 5.
4. Benjamin Richard Pollack, *Becoming Jack LaLanne* (Ph.D. Diss., University of Texas at Austin, 2018).

Ancient Physical Culture(s)

1. E.C. Marchant, Xenophon *Ii. Libri Socratici* (Oxford: Oxford Classical Texts, 1963), 3:12.
2. Taking inspiration from Lukas De Blois and Robartus Johannes Van Der Spek's *An Introduction to the Ancient World* (Routledge, 2008), the term Ancient World will be used to describe the period c. 3000 BCE to 400 CE.
3. Nigel B. Crowther, *Sport in Ancient Times* (Westport: Greenwood Publishing Group, 2007), 1-3.
4. Mike Speak, 'Recreation and Sport in Ancient China,' in James Riordan and Robin Jones, eds., *Sport and Physical Education in China* (London: E & FN Spon, 1999), 28-30.
5. Zhi Dao, *History of Sports in China* (Delhi: DeepLogic, 2019), 56-62.
6. Hai-sheng, Q. I. N., 'The Research on the Weightlifting Sports of Ancient China,' *Journal of Anyang Institute of Technology* 2 (2012): 26.
7. Dao, *History of Sports in China*, 56-62.
8. Lim SK, *Origins of Chinese Sports* (Singapore: Asiapac, 2019), 51-55.
9. Ibid.
10. John A. Wilson, *The Culture of Ancient Egypt* (Chicago: University of Chicago, 2013), 52.
11. Mario C.D. Paganini,. *Gymnasia and Greek Identity in Ptolemaic Egypt* (Oxford: Oxford University Press, 2021).
12. Marley Brown, 'Emblems for the Afterlife,' *Archaeology* 71, no. 3 (2018): 48-53.
13. Wilson Chacko Jacob, *Working out Egypt: Effendi Masculinity and Subject Formation in Colonial Modernity, 1870–1940* (Durham: Duke University Press, 2011), 1-12.

14. Lisa K. Sabbahy, *Daily Life of Women in Ancient Egypt* (London: ABC-CLIO, 2022), 85.
15. Alan Stuart Radley, *The Illustrated History of Physical Culture* (Brighton: Alan Radley, 2001), 4.
16. Roy J. Shephard, *An Illustrated History of Health and Fitness, from Pre-History to Our Post-Modern World* (Toronto: Springer Publishing, 2015), 87.
17. Rosalind O'Hanlon, 'Military Sports and the History of the Martial Body in India,' *Journal of the Economic and Social History of the Orient* 50, no. 4 (2007): 490-523.
18. Melody L. Schoenfeld and Brad Schoenfeld, 'Increasing Strength and Power with Gada, Indian Clubs, Bulgarian Bags, and Other Tools of Concentric Strength,' *Strength and Conditioning Journal* 39, no. 1 (2017): 48-56.
19. Soma Basu, Warfare in Ancient India: An Historical Outline (Delhi: D.K. Printworld, 2014), 205.
20. Nanditha Krishna, *The Book of Vishnu* (Gurgaon: Penguin Books India, 2009), 25–26.
21. Philip Lutgendorf, *Hanumans Tale: The Messages of a Divine Monkey* (Oxford: Oxford University Press, 2006), 1-20.
22. O'Hanlon, 'Military Sports and the History of the Martial Body in India.'
23. Joseph S. Alter, *The Wrestler's Body: Identity and Ideology in North India* (California: University of California Press, 1992), 61.
24. Ibid.
25. James Mallinson and Mark Singleton, *Roots of Yoga* (London: Penguin, 2017), 2-5.
26. Paramhansa Yogananda, *The Essence of the Bhagavad Gita: Explained by Paramhansa Yogananda as Remembered by His Disciple, Swami Kriyananda* (California: Crystal Clarity Publishers, 2008), 67.
27. Kaveh Farrokh, *The Armies of Ancient Persia: The Sassanians* (Barnsley: Pen and Sword, 2014), 15-20.
28. For a comprehensive history see Josiah Ober, *The Rise and Fall of Classical Greece* (New York: Princeton University Press, 2015).
29. Jan Todd, 'From Milo to Milo: A History of Barbells, Dumbbells, and Indian Clubs,' *Iron Game History 3*, no. 6 (1995): 4-16.
30. Humfrey Michell, *Sparta* (Cambridge: Cambridge University Press, 1964), 165.
31. Shephard, *An Illustrated History of Health and Fitness,* 189-191.
32. Jan Todd, 'As Men Do Walk a Mile, Women Should Talk an Hour . . .Tis Their Exercise, and Other Pre-Enlightenment Thought on Women and Purposive Exercise,' *Iron Game History* 7 (2002): 60.
33. Ibid.
34. Ibid.
35. On preparing for the Olympics see Nigel B. Crowther, 'Athlete and State: Qualifying for the Olympic Games in Ancient Greece,' *Journal of Sport History* 23, no. 1 (1996): 34-43.
36. Clayton Miles Lehmann, 'Early Greek Athletic Trainers,' *Journal of Sport History* 36, no. 2 (2009): 187-204.
37. Nigel B. Crowther, 'Weightlifting in Antiquity: Achievement and Training,' *Greece & Rome* 24, no. 2 (1977): 111-120.
38. Todd, 'As Men Do Walk a Mile, Women Should Talk an Hour,' 59.
39. Ibid.
40. Allen Guttmann, *Women's Sports. A History* (New York: Columbia University Press, 1991), 22.
41. Stephen Gaylord Miller, *Ancient Greek Athletics* (London: Yale University Press, 2004), 191.
42. C.A. Forbes, *Greek Physical Education* (London: Century, 1929), 1-12.
43. Clayton Miles Lehmann, 'Early Greek Athletic Trainers,' *Journal of Sport History* 36, no. 2 (2009): 194.
44. Jason P. Shurley, Jan Todd, and Terry Todd, *Strength Coaching in America* (Austin: University of Texas Press, 2021), 12.

Notes

45 Crowther, 'Weightlifting in Antiquity.'
46 Katherine E. Welch, *The Roman Amphitheatre: From its Origins to the Colosseum* (Cambridge: Cambridge University Press, 2007), 14-15.
47 Ibid., 18-20.
48 Ibid.
49 Donald G. Kyle, *Sport and Spectacle in the Ancient World* (London: John Wiley & Sons, 2014), 257-261.
50 Ibid.
51 Anna McCullough, 'Female Gladiators in Imperial Rome: Literary Context and Historical Fact,' *Classical World* 101, no. 2 (2008): 197-209.
52 Shurley, Todd, and Todd, *Strength Coaching in America,* 13.
53 Steven Murray, 'Female Gladiators of the Ancient Roman World,' *Journal of Combative Sport* 7, no. 3 (2003): 1-16.
54 Ian Bradley, *Health, Hedonism and Hypochondria: The Hidden History of Spas* (London: Tauris Parke, 2021), 53.
55 Jack W. Berryman, 'Motion and Rest: Galen on Exercise and Health,' *The Lancet* 380, no. 9838 (2012): 210-211.
56 Ibid.

Disappearance and Re-Emergence

1 Robert A. Mechikoff and Steven Estes, *A History and Philosophy of Sport and Physical Education: From Ancient Civilizations to the Modern World* (New York: McGraw-Hill, 1998), 87.
2 Earle F. Zeigler, *Socio-Cultural Foundations of Physical Education & Educational Sport* (Aachen: Meyer & Meyer Verlag, 2003), 58.
3 Noah Guynn, *Allegory and Sexual Ethics in the High Middle Ages* (New York: Springer, 2007), 49.
4 Sally ED. Wilkins, *Sports and Games of Medieval Cultures* (Connecticut: Greenwood Publishing Group, 2002), 25-55. Colf was a precursor to golf, played with wooden balls and sticks on public streets rather than courses. Real tennis was an early form of what we would call court tennis.
5 Paul B. Newman, *Growing up in the Middle Ages* (Jefferson: McFarland, 2007), 234-235.
6 Jan Todd, *Physical Culture and the Body Beautiful: Purposive Exercise in the Lives of American Women, 1800-1870* (Macon: Mercer University Press, 1998), 83.
7 Jean Froissart, *Les Chroniques de sire Jean Froissart: Qui Traitent des Merveilleuses Emprises, Nobles Aventures et Faits d'armes Advenus en Son Temps en France, Angleterre, Bretaigne, Bourgogne, Escosse, Espaigne, Portingal et ès Autres Parties* (Paris: Auguste Desrez, 1840), 563-564.
8 Jonathan Riley-Smith, *The First Crusade and the Idea of Crusading* (Pennsylvania: University of Pennsylvania Press, 1986), 12-22.
9 Sophie Harwood, *Medieval Women and War: Female Roles in the Old French Tradition* (New York: Bloomsbury Publishing, 2020), 95.
10 Jerry Brotton, *The Renaissance Bazaar: From the Silk Road to Michelangelo* (Oxford: Oxford University Press, 2003), 33-61.
11 Timothy Venning, *A Chronology of the Crusades* (London: Routledge, 2015), 356-360.
12 Sverre Bagge, 'Medieval and Renaissance Historiography: Break or Continuity?' *The European Legacy* 2, no. 8 (1997): 1336-1371.
13 Mechikoff and Estes, *A History and Philosophy of Sport and Physical Education*, 119.
14 Peter C. McIntosh, *Landmarks in the History of Physical Education* (London: Routledge, 2013), 68.

15. Roy J. Shephard, *An Illustrated History of Health and Fitness, from Pre-History to Our Post-Modern World* (Toronto: Springer Publishing, 2015), 413.
16. Ibid.
17. Steven Shapin, 'Was Luigi Cornaro a Dietary Expert?' *Journal of the History of Medicine and Allied Sciences* 73, no. 2 (2018): 135-149.
18. P. C. McIntosh, 'Hieronymus Mercurialis 'De Arte Gymnastica': Classification and Dogma in Physical Education in the Sixteenth Century,' *The International Journal of the History of Sport* 1, no. 1 (1984): 73-84.
19. 'Male Gymnasts Climbing Ropes,' Engraving De arte Gymnastica Girolamo Mercuriale Published: 1672. Wellcome Library, London. Wellcome Images/http://wellcomeimages.org.
20. Roberta J. Park, 'Embodied Selves: The Rise and Development of Concern for Physical Education, Active Games and Recreation for American Women, 1776-1865,' *Journal of Sport History* 5, no. 2 (1978): 21.
21. Todd, *Physical Culture and the Body Beautiful*, 11-14.
22. Ibid., 175-180.
23. Jean-Jacques Rousseau and William H. Payne, *Rousseau's Emile or Treatise on Education* (New York: D. Appleton & Company, 1893), 22.
24. Jennifer J. Popiel, *Rousseau's Daughters: Domesticity, Education, and Autonomy in Modern France* (New Hampshire: UPNE, 2008), 90.
25. Robert Batchelor, 'Thinking about the Gym: Greek Ideals, Newtonian Bodies and Exercise in Early Eighteenth-Century Britain,' *Journal for Eighteenth-Century Studies* 35, no. 2 (2012): 185-197.
26. Terence Todd, *The History of Resistance Exercise and Its Role in United States Education* (Ph.D. diss. The University of Texas, Austin, 1966), 36-38.
27. 'One Ton Lift,' IMDB. Accessed 8 September 2021, https://www.imdb.com/title/tt10703848/.
28. John H. Appleby, 'Human curiosities and the Royal Society, 1699-1751,' *Notes and Records of the Royal Society of London* 50, no. 1 (1996): 13-27.
29. Jan Todd, 'The Classical Ideal and Its Impact on the Search for Suitable Exercise: 1774–1830,' *Iron Game History* 2, no. 4 (1992): 7-16.
30. George Forrest, *A Handbook of Gymnastics* (Routledge: London, 1862), 9-10.
31. Duygu Harmandar Demirel and Ibrahim Yildiran, 'The Philosophy of Physical Education and Sport from Ancient Times to the Enlightenment,' *European Journal of Educational Research* 2, no. 4 (2013): 191-202.

The Birth of Physical Culture

1. A. Wallace Jones, *Fifty Exercises for Health & Strength* (London: Health & Strength Ltd., c. 1908), 9.
2. Fred Eugene Leonard, A Guide to the History of Physical Education (Lea & Febiger: Philadelphia, 1923), 120.
3. Michael Adams, *Napoleon and Russia* (London: A&C Black, 2014), 93.
4. Richard Kraus, *Recreation and Leisure in Modern Society* (New Jersey: Prentice-Hall, 1971), 175.
5. Michael Krüger, 'The History of German Sports Clubs: Between Integration and Emigration,' *The International Journal of the History of Sport* 30, no. 14 (2013): 1586-1603.
6. John M. Hoberman, *Sport and Political Ideology* (Austin: University of Texas Press, 1984), 58.
7. Gertrud Pfister, 'The Role of German Turners in American Physical Education,' *The International Journal of the History of Sport* 26, no. 13 (2009): 1893-1925.
8. Annette R. Hofmann, 'Lady Turners in the United States: German American Identity,

Gender Concerns, and Turnerism,' *Journal of Sport History* 27, no. 3 (2000): 383-404.
9. Suzanne Lundvall, 'From Ling Gymnastics to Sport Science: The Swedish School of Sport and Health Sciences, GIH, from 1813 to 2013,' *The International Journal of The History of Sport* 32, no. 6 (2015): 789-799.
10. Samantha Melnick, 'Per Henrik Ling-Pioneer of Physiotherapy and Gymnastics,' *European Journal of Physical Education and Sport Science* 1, no. 1 (2016): 13-19.
11. Claire Nolte, *The Sokol in the Czech Lands to 1914: Training for the Nation* (New York: Springer, 2002).
12. Jesper Andreasson and Thomas Johansson, 'The Fitness Revolution: Historical Transformations in the Global Gym and Fitness Culture,' *Sport science review* 23, no. 3-4 (2014): 91-112.
13. Jan Todd, *Physical Culture and the Body Beautiful: Purposive Exercise in the lives of American Women, 1800-1870* (Macon: Mercer University Press, 1998), 30-45.
14. Ibid., 76-80.
15. Ibid., 66.
16. Ibid., 158.
17. Ibid., 150-154.
18. Ann Chisholm, 'Incarnations and Practices of Feminine Rectitude: Nineteenth-Century Gymnastics for US Women,' *Journal of Social History* 38, no. 3 (2005): 737-763.
19. Todd, *Physical Culture and the Body Beautiful,* 220-228.
20. Ibid.
21. Mary F. Eastman, *The Biography of Dio Lewis* (New York: Fowler & Wells Company, 1891), 81-84.
22. Conor Heffernan, 'Indian Club Wwinging in the Early Victorian Period,' *Sport in History* 37, no. 1 (2017): 95-120.
23. Nikolai Bogdanovic, *Fit to Fight: A History of the Royal Army Physical Training Corps 1860–2015* (London: Bloomsbury Publishing, 2017), 13-16.
24. Martha H. Verbrugge, *Able-Bodied Womanhood: Personal Health and Social Change in Nineteenth-Century Boston* (New York: Oxford University Press, 1988), 8 & 195.
25. The foundational text in this regard is Patricia Vertinsky, *The Eternally Wounded Woman: Women, Doctors, and Exercise in the Late Nineteenth Century* (Manchester: Manchester University Press, 1990).
26. Roberta J. Park, 'Embodied Selves: The Rise and Development of Concern for Physical Education, Active Games and Recreation for American Women, 1776-1865,' *Journal of Sport History* 5, no. 2 (1978): 5-41.
27. Heffernan, 'Indian Club Wwinging in the Early Victorian Period.'
28. Jan Todd, 'Strength is Health: George Barker Windship and the First American Weight Training Boom,' *Iron Game History* 3, no. 1 (1993): 3-14.
29. Jan Todd, 'Reflections on Physical Culture. Defining Our Field and Protecting Its Integrity,' *Iron Game History* 13, no. 2-3 (2015): 5.
30. The quintessential Sandow biography remains David L. Chapman's, *Sandow the Magnificent: Eugen Sandow and the Beginnings of Bodybuilding* (Chicago: University of Illinois Press, 1994).
31. Carolyn De la Peña, 'Dudley Allen Sargent: Health Machines and the Energized Male Body.' *Iron Game History* 8, no. 2 (2003): 3-19.
32. Again, see Chapman, *Sandow the Magnificent.*
33. Kimberly Ayn Beckwith, *Building Strength: Alan Calvert, the Milo Bar-bell Company, and the Modernization of American Weight Training* (PhD. Diss, The University of Texas at Austin, 2006).
34. Jan Todd, Kim Beckwith, 'Strength: America's First Muscle Magazine 1914-1935, *Iron Game History* 9, no. 1 (2005): 11-28.
35. Jan Todd, 'Bernarr Macfadden: Reformer of Feminine Form,' *Journal of Sport History* 14, no. 1 (1987): 61-75.

36. David Chapman and Patricia Vertinsky, *Venus with Biceps: A Pictorial History of Muscular Women* (Vancouver: Arsenal Pulp Press, 2010), 1-22.
37. Sheila Fletcher, *Women First: The Female Tradition in English Physical Education, 1880–1980* (Dover: Athlone, 1984); Kathleen E. McCrone, *Playing the Game: Sport and the Physical Emancipation of English Women, 1870-1914* (Kentucky: University Press of Kentucky, 1988).
38. Two great introductory texts on women's sport are Jennifer Hargreaves, *Sporting Females: Critical Issues in the History and Sociology of Women's Sport* (London: Routledge, 2002): Jean Williams, *A Contemporary History of Women's Sport, Part One: Sporting Women, 1850-1960* (London: Routledge, 2014).
39. Malissa Smith, *A History of Women's Boxing* (Lanham: Rowman & Littlefield, 2014), 1-22.
40. Verbrugge, *Able-Bodied Womanhood*, 5-33.
41. Todd, 'Bernarr Macfadden: Reformer of Feminine Form.'
42. Gherardo Bonini, 'London: The Cradle of Modern Weightlifting,' *Sports Historian* 21, no. 1 (2001): 56-70.
43. Mark Singleton, *Yoga Body: The Origins of Modern Posture Practice* (Oxford: Oxford University Press, 2010), 113-162.
44. Aishwarya Ramachandran and Conor Heffernan, 'A Distinctly Indian body? KV Iyer and Physical Culture in 1930s India,' *The International Journal of the History of Sport* 36, no. 12 (2019): 1053-1075.
45. Alessio Ponzio, *Shaping the New Man: Youth Training Regimes in Fascist Italy and Nazi Germany* (Wisconsin: University of Wisconsin Pres, 2015).
46. Mike O'Mahony, *Sport in the USSR: Physical Culture—Visual Culture* (London: Reaktion books, 2006).
47. Charlotte Macdonald, *Strong, Beautiful and Modern: National Fitness in Britain, New Zealand, Australia and Canada, 1935-1960* (Vancouver: UBC Press, 2013), 5-14.
48. Jill Julius Matthews, 'They Had Such a Lot of Fun: The Women's League of Health and Beauty between the Wars,' *History Workshop Journal* 30, no. 1 (1990): 22-54.
49. John D. Fair, 'The Tragic History of the Military Press in Olympic and World Championship Competition, 1928-1972,' *Journal of Sport History* 28, no. 3 (2001): 345-374.
50. Benjamin Pollack and Janice Todd, 'Before Charles Atlas: Earle Liederman, the 1920s King of Mail-Order Muscle,' *Journal of Sport History* 44, no. 3 (2017): 399-420.
51. Jacqueline Reich, 'The World's Most Perfectly Developed Man: Charles Atlas, Physical Culture, and the Inscription of American Masculinity,' *Men and Masculinities* 12, no. 4 (2010): 444-461.
52. Penelope Latey, 'The Pilates Method: History and Philosophy,' *Journal of Bodywork and Movement Therapies* 5, no. 4 (2001): 275-282.
53. John D. Fair, *Mr. America: The Tragic History of a Bodybuilding Icon* (Austin: University of Texas Press, 2015), 1-33.
54. A wonderful biography of Hoffman and his legacy is John D. Fair's, *Muscletown USA: Bob Hoffman and the Manly Culture of York Barbell* (Pennsylvania: Penn State Press, 1999).

The Age of Fitness

1. Jane Fonda, *Jane Fonda's Workout Book* (New York: Simon & Schuster, 1981), 12.
2. Randy Roach, *Muscle, Smoke, and Mirrors* (Bloomington: AuthorHouse, 2008), xix.
3. Elsa Devienne, 'The Life, Death, and Rebirth of Muscle Beach: Reassessing the Muscular Physique in Postwar America, 1940s–1980s,' *Southern California Quarterly* 100, no. 3 (2018): 324-367.
4. Jan Todd, 'The Origins of Weight Training for Female Athletes in North America,' *Iron*

Notes

Game History 2, no. 2 (1992): 4-14.

5. This is retold in Joe Weider, Ben Weider, and Mike Steere. *Brothers of Iron* (Danville: Sports Publishing LLC, 2006), 59-84.
6. Hoffman brought the US to the 1936, 1948, 1952, 1956, and 1960 Olympic Games. The 1940 Olympic Games, scheduled for Tokyo, Japan, and then Helsinki, Finland, were cancelled due to the outbreak of the Second World War (1939-1945).
7. John D. Fair, *Muscletown USA: Bob Hoffman and the Manly Culture of York Barbell* (Pennsylvania: Penn State Press, 1999), 107-154.
8. Jason Shurley, 'Unequaled Yet Never Equal: The Portrayal of John Davis in Strength & Health Magazine,' *Iron Game History* 13/14, nos. 4/1 (2016): 38-53.
9. John D. Fair, 'Isometrics or steroids? Exploring new frontiers of strength in the early 1960s,' *Journal of Sport History* 20, no. 1 (1993): 1-24.
10. Randy Roach, *Muscle, Smoke, and Mirrors* (Bloomington: AuthorHouse, 2008), 335.
11. A wonderful early history of the supplement industry is Daniel T. Hall and John D. Fair's, 'The Pioneers of Protein,' *Iron Game History* 8, no. 3 (2004): 23-34.
12. John D. Fair, *Mr. America: The Tragic History of a Bodybuilding Icon* (Austin: University of Texas Press, 2015), 157-194.
13. A term used to describe a period of political hostility between the United States and the Soviet Union and their respective allies, the Cold War lasted from 1947 to 1991.
14. Matthew T. Bowers and Thomas M. Hunt, 'The President's Council on Physical Fitness and the Systematisation of Children's play in America,' *The International Journal of the History of Sport* 28, no. 11 (2011): 1496-1511.
15. Robert H. Boyle, 'The Report that Shocked the President,' *Sports Illustrated* 3, no. 15 (1955): 30-33.
16. Dave Day and Samantha-Jayne Oldfield, 'Delineating Professional and Amateur Athletic Bodies in Victorian England,' *Sport in History* 35, no. 1 (2015): 19-45.
17. Shelly McKenzie, *Getting Physical: The Rise of Fitness Culture in America* (Lawrence: University Press of Kansas, 2013), 109-145.
18. Alan Latham, 'The History of a Habit: Jogging as a Palliative to Sedentariness in 1960s America,' *Cultural Geographies* 22, no. 1 (2015): 103-126.
19. Although not all sports received an uptake in funding and support. American football is one obvious example.
20. Jan Todd and Désirée Harguess, 'Doris Barrilleaux and the Beginnings of Modern Women's Bodybuilding,' *Iron Game History* 11, no. 4 (2012): 7-21.
21. For a very in-depth discussion of women's Olympic weightlifting, see V. Panayotov and N. Yankova, 'Retrospective Analysis of Achievements of Women Weightlifters at the Olympic Games,' *Trakia Journal of Sciences* 18, no. 1 (2020): 918-923.
22. This is all covered in John D. Fair and David L. Chapman's, *Muscles in the Movies: Perfecting the Art of Illusion* (Missouri: University of Missouri Press, 2020).
23. Alan M. Klein, *Little Big Men: Bodybuilding Subculture and Gender Construction* (New York: Suny Press, 1993), 1-23.
24. Randy Roach, *Muscle, Smoke, and Mirrors* (Vancouver: AuthorHouse, 2008), 376-378.
25. Ben Pollack and Jan Todd, 'American Icarus: Vic Tanny and America's First Health Club Chain,' *Iron Game History,* 13/14, nos. 4/1 (2016): 17-37.
26. Randy Roach, *Muscle, Smoke, and Mirrors* (Vancouver: AuthorHouse, 2011).
27. Jason P. Shurley, Jan Todd, and Terry Todd, *Strength Coaching in America* (Austin: University of Texas Press, 2021), 129-156.
28. Louise Mansfield, "Sexercise': Working Out Heterosexuality in Jane Fonda's Fitness Books,' *Leisure Studies* 30, no. 2 (2011): 237-255.
29. Suzanne Newcombe and Phillip Deslippe, 'Anglophone Yoga and Meditation Inside and Outside of India,' in Suzanne Newcombe and Karen O'Brien-Kop (eds.) *Routledge Handbook of Yoga and Meditation Studies* (London: Routledge, 2020), 458-465.
30. Singleton, *Yoga Body,* 176-200.

31. Christina Gough, 'Health & Fitness Clubs - Statistics & Facts,' *Statistica,* March 10, 2021. Accessed September 28, 2021, https://www.statista.com/topics/1141/health-and-fitness-clubs/
32. 'Industry Statistics: Global Dietary Supplements Market Size Will Grow to USD 306.8 Billion by 2026, Says Facts & Factors,' *Intrado,* January 10, 2021. Accessed September 28, 2021, https://www.globenewswire.com/news-release/2021/01/19/2160500/0/en/Industry-Statistics-Global-Dietary-Supplements-Market-Size-Will-Grow-to-USD-306-8-Billion-by-2026-Says-Facts-Factors.html.
33. Thomas W. Buford, Richard B. Kreider, Jeffrey R. Stout, Mike Greenwood, Bill Campbell, Marie Spano, Tim Ziegenfuss, Hector Lopez, Jamie Landis, and Jose Antonio, 'International Society of Sports Nutrition Position Stand: Creatine Supplementation and Exercise,' *Journal of the International Society of Sports Nutrition* 4, no. 1 (2007): 1-8.
34. Daniel Lukas Rosenke, 'Supply and Enhance: Tracing the Doping Supply Chain in the 1980s,' (University of Texas at Austin: PhD diss., 2020), 197-239.
35. Adrian Wilairat, 'Faster, Higher, Stronger-Federal Efforts to Criminalize Anabolic Steroids and Steroid Precursors,' *J. Health Care L. & Pol'y* 8 (2005): 377.
36. Pieter A. Cohen, John C. Travis, and Bastiaan J. Venhuis. 'A Methamphetamine Analog (N, α-diethyl-phenylethylamine) Identified in a Mainstream Dietary Supplement,' *Drug Testing and Analysis* 6, no. 7-8 (2014): 805-807.
37. Harrison Pope, Katharine A. Phillips, and Roberto Olivardia, *The Adonis Complex: The Secret Crisis of Male Body Obsession* (New York: Simon and Schuster, 2000).
38. Leslie Heywood, *Bodymakers: A Cultural Anatomy of Women's Body Building* (New Jersey: Rutgers University Press, 1998), 1-20.
39. Shelly A. McGrath, and Ruth A. Chananie-Hill, '"Big Freaky-Looking Women": Normalizing Gender Transgression through Bodybuilding,' *Sociology of Sport Journal* 26, no. 2 (2009): 235-254.
40. On CrossFit as a movement, see Marcelle C. Dawson, 'CrossFit: Fitness Cult or Reinventive Institution?' *International Review for the Sociology of Sport* 52, no. 3 (2017): 361-379.
41. BIPOC, meaning Black, Indigenous and People of Color. On the Glassman controversy, see Shannon L. Walsh, *Eugenics and Physical Culture Performance in the Progressive Era* (New York: Palgrave Macmillan, 2020), 189-195.
42. Mair Underwood, 'Exploring the Social Lives of Image and Performance Enhancing Drugs: An Online Ethnography of the Zyzz Fandom of Recreational Bodybuilders,' *International Journal of Drug Policy* 39 (2017): 78-85.

The Past, Present and Future of Physical Culture

1. Niall Richardson, 'What is the Practice of Bodybuilding?' in Niall Richardson and Adam Locks (eds.), *Critical Readings in Bodybuilding* (London: Routledge, 2013), 1.
2. World Health Organization, *Global action plan on physical activity 2018-2030: more active people for a healthier world* (Geneva: World Health Organization, 2019).
3. Alfred Danks, *Danks System of Physical Culture* (London: Alfred Danks, 1933), xi.

www.ingramcontent.com/pod-product-compliance
Lightning Source LLC
Chambersburg PA
CBHW022138160426
43197CB00009B/1345